Daniela Vallega Neu

2-21-2011

# The Bodily Dimension in Thinking

SUNY series in Contemporary Continental Philosophy

Denis J. Schmidt, editor

# The Bodily Dimension in Thinking

*Daniela Vallega-Neu*

State University of New York Press

Published by
State University of New York Press, Albany

For information, address State University of New York Press,
194 Washington Avenue, Suite 305, Albany, NY 12210-2384

Production by Judith Block
Marketing by Michael Campochiaro


**Library of Congress Cataloging-in-Publication Data**

Vallega-Neu, Daniela, 1966–
    The bodily dimension in thinking / Daniela Vallega-Neu.
        p. cm. — (SUNY series in contemporary continental philosophy)
    Includes bibliographical references and index.
    ISBN 0-7914-6561-6 (hardcover : alk. paper) — ISBN 0-7914-6562-4
    (pbk. : alk. paper)
    1. Body, Human (philosophy)   2. Mind and body.   I. Title.   II. Series.

    B.105.B64V35  2005
    128'.6—dc22
                                                                    2004029607

10 9 8 7 6 5 4 3 2 1

For Alejandro

*Für den Schaffenden gilt immer noch, was für Dante galt:*
*Der Körper . . . ist für ihn die Seele.*
*(Rilke über Rodin's Zeichnungen)*

For the one who creates still holds what was true for Dante:
The body . . . is for him the soul.
(Rilke on Rodin's drawings)

# Contents

# Preface

During my studies in Freiburg I found myself saying to a friend that if there is one thing I could say about truth this was that it hits its target ("Wahrheit trifft"). What I had in mind when I was saying this was not a concept or an idea of truth but a certain corporeal experience that goes along with thinking when an event or thought exhibits a certain creative and transformative power. Of course, this corporeal experience is not always the same, but it marks a site for thought that I have been seeking and enjoying since my first early and tentative attempts in the field of philosophy. What does not pass through that site remains for me on a philosophical level unintelligible and uninteresting. This experience of a corporeal site of thinking is what guides the explorations of this book.

The project for this book arose during my last year in Freiburg (1995) and since then I have worked on it in many places (Freiburg and Jena in Germany, Travedona and Città di Castello in Italy, State College and Turlock in the United States). I first presented this project for the application to a postdoctoral fellowship from the Deutscher Akademischer Austausch Dienst (DAAD) in order to work with Charles Scott and John Sallis at Penn State University and was granted this fellowship for the academic year 1997–1998. I thank Charles Scott and John Sallis, whose work since then has been a precious source of inspiration for me, for their continuous support and comments on my work. I presented some of the chapters of this book at conferences in various places (University of Jena, *Collegium Phaenomenologicum* in Città di Castello, Heidegger Conference of America, Western Phenomenology Conference) and I am grateful for the feedback I received from various colleagues and friends on these occasions. Susan Schoenbohm helped me especially with the initial chapters of the book, and I also thank Omar Rivera for reading the whole manuscript and for making editorial corrections and thoughtful comments that helped me strengthen many ideas. Further I am grateful to James Risser and to Linda Neu for their continuous support. In particular, I thank Alejandro A. Vallega who was always there for me as an engaging interlocutor, thoughtful reader, and supporting companion.

Travedona, August 14, 2004

# Introduction

Since its Greek beginnings, Western philosophy has been characterized in its most proper activity as thinking reflecting on itself, and this self-reflection has been characterized as a move away from the body. It appears that body and thinking acquire their proper determinations in their distinction and opposition. Certainly, the philosophers of our tradition are well aware that this move away from the body is not a real separation, since all reflection we perform as living beings inevitably remains tied to the body, but nevertheless many from them still conceive thinking as an activity that is radically different from the body and its life. More recently, following Nietzsche, many attempts have been made to articulate the activity of thinking not in distinction or opposition to the body but as itself "bodily." But even Nietzsche contended that the moment we think the body, this body becomes an object of thought that is never able to adequately represent the lived body prior to its categorization in thought. Since traditional determinations of the body arise precisely in their distinction to thinking and concepts of thought, the question arises whether this move away from the body is an inevitable consequence of reflexive thought, and whether it is at all possible to think the body reflexively without objectifying it. My claim is that this is possible, but in order to do this we may have to abandon certain preconceptions of what the body is and of how thinking occurs. One way to question and undermine the traditional mind-body dualism is to discover and articulate how thinking itself is a bodily event. When attempting to explore the bodily aspect of thought, as it is revealed to us in reflexive thought, we first need to question what we mean here by "body." Thus, one main question of this book is: *How are we to think the "body" that we find at play in our own thought?*

This question already implies a certain access to whatever is designated here as "body." The body in question is not taken as a posited thing, as an object of scientific inquiry at which I can look from a distance. Rather it is found or discovered in a reflective experience. Such reflective experience must not necessarily be of philosophical nature. Different forms of reflective experiences of the body are for instance required in the performing arts (dancing, acting) and in various forms of meditation. Similarly to how a dancer as she dances remains conscious of the movements of her body in such a way that this body is not objectified, in philosophical inquiries thinking may remain alert to the bodily movements that are at play *as* this thinking occurs. The difficulty here is to find a form of reflection as well as a language that do not simply objectify the occurrences that they address.

To question reflexively the body through which or in which our thoughts take shape implies that the body in question is not already there for thought but first comes to be for thought in thought—that is, performatively. In attuned and attentive awareness of what we may come to call "bodily" movements in thinking, body emerges as an occurrence and dimension that characterizes and shapes the very thought in which it emerges. This implies that the emerging of the body does not resolve in a full presence of a body-thing that becomes an object of thought. Rather, body emerges opaquely in its coming to pass as a temporal dimension that carries innumerable concrete and singular articulations of thought. Thus, what allows us to thematize the bodily dimension in thought is the attention to the emergence of thought as a bodily event. This addresses a second main question of this book that concerns the arising of thought and that complements the previous question: *How do we* come to *think the "body" that we find at play in our own thought?*

When we attempt to stay alert to the bodily aspects or qualities that we experience in the emergence of our thoughts we do not find a "body-object" that is already there. At first, what we may experience are movements, desires, resistances, directionalities, shapes, and images; occurrences that Descartes attributes to what he calls the thinking substance precisely in opposition to the body conceived as an extended substance. This may raise the question whether we can properly speak of a "body" when we attempt to describe the sensations, desires, resistances, and movements at play in the enactment of thought. Is a body not by definition a thing, an object of thought, and like every object of thought the result of a complicated process we call thinking? Have we not been trained too well by our tradition to understand bodies in opposition to conscious thought as this mute impenetrable mass of organs, tissues, bones, and skin? Would we not be misled by continuing to speak of body when referring to this sensible dimension of thought? "Why not speak of 'physicality,' or 'sensibility,' or 'flesh'?" a friend once asked me. I have thought about this question since and about why I am not ready to abandon this word, "body," all together.

I am aware that when I look reflexively for the body that I find at play in the enactment of thought, strictly speaking, I do not find a thing. What I find are occurrences, motions, densities, which in fact leads me to speak not of "the body" in thought but rather of the "bodily dimension" in thought or the way in which thought "*occurs* bodily." In some instances I may also speak of the physicality of thought, or of its sensibility, or, with Merleau-Ponty, of its flesh. I believe that the advantage of staying with word forms related to "body" is that, in doing so, we may have a sense of a temporal and spatial concreteness and singularity that I do not find in the same way in the word "physicality." Further, the word physicality, to my ear, carries more scientific connotations and with these a sense of objectivity that would hinder my explorations of bodily being and thinking. Had I written this book in German, I would have used the term "*Leib*,"[1] which in phenomenology has come to designate the lived body, and not the term "*Körper*," which designates any body-object in a larger sense; that is, living and inanimate "bodies" that we perceive in outer perception and that as such become objects of scientific inquiry. In speaking of the body, I am concerned with the lived body (Leib) that we *are* and that reveals itself in a strange intimacy, as we remain alert to its motions in thinking.

This does not mean that I simply question the body subjectively and not objectively. Such a reading would not only be an oversimplification but it would also be misleading. As I will show, the exploration of the bodily quality of thinking leads to a "desubjectivation" of thought with respect to the Western tradition, in that it points to the physical interweaving of thinking and other bodies and physical events. Once we focus on how bodies play in thought we can no longer understand thinking simply as the activity of a subject, nor can we understand thinking as an activity that is somehow opposed to a world and objects it thinks. The bodily dimension in thought points to how thinking is *of* the world, said with Merleau-Ponty's words, it points to how thinking shares the flesh of the world, and to how its texture is woven into histories that reach farther than our "subjectivity" and our conscious memories.[2] This is why I prefer not to speak of the bodily dimension *of* thought, which would suggest that the bodily dimension in question belongs primarily to thinking. In opposition to this, I believe that thinking belongs to this bodily dimension that reaches beyond what we may come to name as "ourselves" and that shapes the very ways in which we come to understand ourselves. The following of the trace of the body in our thought reveals the strangers we are to ourselves, but may also lead to a new understanding of how we come to be who we are in relation to the world we live in.

This book is composed of a series of studies of philosophical texts, in which I explore how Plato, Nietzsche, Scheler, Merleau-Ponty, Heidegger, and Foucault think of bodies, and how in the way they think of bodies possibilities are opened to conceive bodies beyond what these philosophers explicitly think. When reading these philosophers I look for both, how they think bodies and how a bodily dimension is at play in their thinking; that is, I look for how determinations of a "body" or "bodies" arise in their thought, and how the enactment of their thought is itself "bodily." This requires that, in reading their texts, the reader stay attuned and alert to the movements and articulations of their thoughts by sharing a strange intimacy with the texts as these unfold in the reading. It is in this attentiveness to *how* the thoughts of the philosophers take shape in their texts that I find determinations of bodily events that may not find explicit articulation in these texts. This reading does not lead to one uniform way of understanding bodies and the bodily dimension in thought. Rather, the presented readings proliferate the ways we understand bodies at the same time that we come to see how bodies take place in articulations of differences that shape the way we are and the way we think. Thus the exploration of the bodily dimension in thinking opens the way to an understanding of bodies not simply as things in space and in time but rather as dimensions through which and in which space and time find articulations always anew in quite singular ways. Ultimately this leads to the possibility of an ontology of bodily being for which this book may present a series of preliminary studies.

The first part of this book explores body and thinking at the limit of metaphysics. The second part explores two phenomenological accounts of the body. The third part explores different ways to think bodies beyond subjectivity. The three parts mark a trajectory from the limits of classical metaphysics to those of phenomenology, and from these to those of an ontology of bodily being. More specifically, the first part discusses the limits of the history of Platonism, with the arising and collapsing of a mind-body dualism in Plato and Nietzsche. The second part explores the bodily dimension in thinking in two phenomenological approaches that, in different ways, lie at the limit of a Husserlian phenomenology: Scheler's phenomenology broaches classical ontology, whereas Merleau-Ponty's phenomenology broaches a postclassical ontology of the flesh. The third part explores the bodily dimension in thinking at the limits of articulations of the singularities of bodies beyond subjectivity: Heidegger opens possibilities to think the singularities of bodies by breaking through subjectivity from within traditional Western philosophy, whereas Foucault breaks through subjectivity at the limit of philosophy through historical analyses of practices and institutions. In each of the philosophers discussed in the three parts we will find different ways of articulating bodies, as well as quite singular forms of bodily thinking.

In a reading of Plato's *Timaeus* (part 1, chapter 1) I will trace the differencing between thinking and body that sets an essential stage for the history of metaphysics and the determinations of body and thinking that follows it. The discussion questions how the distinction between a realm of the intelligi-

ble and of the sensible comes to be in and for thinking and traces this distinction back to *legein*, a term I understand to indicate a bodily activity of differencing and gathering that at its source withdraws from conceptualization. The
second chapter comprises a reading of Nietzsche and shows how in his work
the difference between body and thinking within metaphysics reaches its limit
and how Nietzsche "twists free" from Platonism. In this chapter I argue that
Nietzsche remains largely imprisoned in a post-Kantian epistemology that
seals the realm of consciousness off from the possibility of conceiving anything
outside of consciousness. To speak of body and thereby reveal the truth of the
body is impossible for Nietzsche, since, when I think of body, the body is already an object of consciousness and thus never reveals what it could truly be
"in itself" prior to becoming an object of thought. However, I will also argue
that Nietzsche does break through this "prison" of consciousness and opens a
bodily dimension of thought in the *performativity* of his thought; that is, in
exposing performatively how thought happens "bodily."

The second part of this book considers how, after the post-Kantian closure of consciousness on itself, phenomenology reopens possibilities to rethink
and articulate the body and the bodily dimension in thought. In chapter 3, after
considering in a brief introduction phenomenology's possibilities for thinking
bodies, I look at the more traditional position of Max Scheler, who maintains
explicitly a distinction between spirit (*Geist*) and what he calls the "vital sphere"
(*Vitalsphäre*), a position that in many ways points back to Plato. The chapter
shows how Scheler avoids a simple objectification of the body when he conceives it as an "analyzer" that determines whether and how one perceives something. I will also argue that his late thought of the "powerlessness of the spirit"
not only leads to an overcoming of the dualism between mind and body, but that
it also puts into question the separate principles Scheler claims for life and spirit.
Yet, even if Scheler thinks the mutual penetration of life and spirit, for him the
issue of this mutual penetration is the enlivening of spirit and not the return of
thinking to its bodily origins. The latter is the project of Merleau-Ponty's
thought, which I consider in chapter 4. In this chapter I focus primarily on
Merleau-Ponty's *The Visible and the Invisible* as well as on his last working notes.
I begin my reading of Merleau-Ponty with a problematization of his attempt to
articulate "brute being" (*être brut*) in the light of traditional reflexive thought.
In this context I further develop the idea of a kind of reflection I call "awareness," which, instead of already objectifying the occurrences that come to our
awareness, goes along with them. Then I follow Merleau-Ponty's ontology of
the flesh from the archetype of reflection in the relation between body and
things to an articulation of thought as recoiling flesh, and finally to an exploration of the gap at the center of the chiasm between flesh of the body and flesh

of the world. He conceives this gap as a negativity that is an articulate opening for a variety of chiasmic relations. I end the chapter with some critical thoughts regarding the question of a certain primacy of perception and a primacy of vision in Merleau-Ponty's work.

The third part of this book explores ways to articulate body and the bodily dimension of thought beyond metaphysics and particularly in the overcoming of subjectivity. My discussion of Heidegger in chapter 5 elaborates further what I call bodily awareness, specifically in connection with the attunements that for Heidegger disclose what gives itself to thought. The discussion shows that in *Contributions to Philosophy* Heidegger allows us to think through specific attunements how the disclosure of being that occurs in being-t/here (*Da-sein*) occurs always bodily. This means both that the disclosure of being occurs with and in things (bodies in the sense of entities) and that being is bodily itself. The way we are and think arises in this bodily articulation of a world. Whereas Heidegger breaks thought subjectivity from within a radicalized philosophical reflection on being, Foucault breaks with it from the outside through an oblique consideration of ways in which power formations at play in institutions and practices shape our bodies and with them our thoughts. Chapter 6 focuses especially on Foucault's later thought of *Discipline and Punish* and *The History of Sexuality*. In his genealogy Foucault performs a "thought from the outside," in which attempts to account for the formation of subjectivities out of embodied lineages of discourses and practices, without recurring to traditional reflexive thought. This approach leads to a questioning of the limits of philosophy, if we understand philosophy as occurring in self-reflexive thinking.

In the concluding part of this book I highlight different aspects from the philosophical texts that the previous chapters consider, in order to indicate how they open possibilities for an ontology of bodily being. I indicate how a sensitivity to the bodily dimension in thinking fosters an engagement with the singularity of things and living beings in a way that leaves them in their own singular happenings at the same time that it encroaches them in movements of attraction, repulsion, resistance, in playfulness and indifference. The sensitivity to the bodily dimension of thought merges into and out of the sensitivity to the bodily dimension of things, living beings, gestures, signs, and words.

A main issue of this book is how an exploration of the bodily dimension in thought leads to a "desubjectivation" of thought; that is, it leads to understanding how thinking arises in the world and not in a somehow separate entity one may call the human mind or soul. It is thus that this book may serve as a preliminary work for an ontology of bodily being. However, the sequence of studies I propose in this book do not simply form an itinerary that leads from the intimacy of the human soul to finding ourselves out there in a world.

Rather, each chapter looks in a variety of philosophical texts for possibilities to conceive thinking as a bodily event arising in the world and in commonality with things. Furthermore, each text I explore sheds a different light on the lived body, or, I may also say, on bodily being in thought.

The choice of philosophers and texts follows two criteria. First, I chose some of the philosophers who appear to me to make major contributions to how to think bodies. Second, I limited myself to philosophers from the Western tradition, which is the tradition in which I was raised and which influences largely contemporary discussions in continental philosophy. I understand my book to perform some groundwork in that it prepares the grounds for transformed ways to understand bodies and thinking. It appears to me that, although issues of body are often raised in contemporary academic philosophy, the work that is done in these fields often falls short of reflections on approaches of thought as well as of careful conceptual work. I also believe that if we want to change ways of thinking that appear limiting to us, we need to rework the history of philosophy that informs our interpretations, and we need to reinterpret this history in such a way that it transforms the way in which it informs our behavior and understanding of matters at hand. Both Heidegger and Foucault show such a concern in their interpretation of history.

The accounts I give in this book are far from being "complete" in the sense that I limit myself to specific texts and that there certainly are more philosophers and works that could make major contributions to the questions I pursue. I believe that some readers will especially miss feminist approaches to the issue of body and thinking or at least consideration of issues of gender, since so much work is being done in this field today. Although in my initial project of this book I had planned to include chapters on issues of gender, I came to think that this would require much more work and possibly another book. However, I believe that, within the limited scope I set for myself in this book, in my consideration of the bodily being in thought the interested reader will find an opening to issues of gender as well as to issues of non-Western thinking. Once we understand not only *that* but especially *how* thinking arises in our bodily being in the world with things, once we form the *habit* to be aware of how this occurs we do not need to look anymore for ways to "open" traditional thought to issues of gender or non-Western thought, since we are aware that we are already out there in the encroachment of lineages and singular lives, most of which remain utterly strange to us. What we would need to learn to do, thus, is to think *out* of this encroachment of lineages and lives that we experience. At best, this book may make some contribution toward forming these habits and, thus, it may open ways to reorient philosophical reflection in ways pertinent to our time.

# PART ONE

# At the Limits of Metaphysics

Plato and Nietzsche mark limits of the history of metaphysics in different ways. In rather simplistic terms, one may say that where Plato initiates a certain dualism between body and thinking, Nietzsche works at dissolving it. However the limits that their philosophies mark are not simply a point of beginning and a point of ending in a linear and uniform history. First, because their thoughts are more thresholds than points, which means that their thoughts demarcate a beginning and an end at the same time. Second, because the history of philosophy that unfolds between Plato and Nietzsche is far from being uniform.

Plato's thought is a threshold in that, even though he makes it an ethical task to gather one's thoughts away from the body, in his dialogues he clearly situates thought concretely in life. Thus, he leads away from understanding thinking as a bodily event at the same time that he opens up a possibility to consider thought as a bodily event. Accordingly, his notion of psyche (soul) retains an ambiguous meaning since, as long as we live, its rational part is bound to its sensitive and emotional part. In a certain sense this notion oscillates between the more "material" understanding of psyche in the pre-Socratics and the later Platonistic positions that tend to understand the soul (and with it thinking) as distinct from the body. The following chapter will concentrate on the motions of the psyche and its occurrence as a differencing that leads to a distinction between body and soul, but I will claim that this differencing itself—that is, the motions of the psyche—is a physical occurrence. This means that I find the bodily dimension of thinking in Plato's text in the motions of the psyche.

Nietzsche is a threshold between neo-Kantian rationalism and a variety of philosophical movements that understand thinking as a bodily occurrence and that aim at an overcoming of metaphysical dualisms. Thus Nietzsche's thinking is delimited by modern thought at the same time that he breaks through its limits by reopening, in a different way from Plato, the possibility to think the bodily dimension in thought. As in Plato, in Nietzsche too the bodily dimension in thought appears in the performativity of the text, although in quite different ways. In Nietzsche, the bodily dimension in thinking finds its articulation less in the emerging of differences than in a going under of traditional differentiations. It is found in the collapse of structures of thought and of values that have become empty corpses for thinking; masks without faces. As is well known, this collapse is for Nietzsche a feast in that in it he finds again possibilities of life.

As regards metaphysics and its history, it does not begin only with Plato nor did it end with Nietzsche. Further, there always have been materialistic positions in philosophy (in the ancient Greeks, in the Middle Ages, in modern and also in contemporary philosophy) that contend that there is nothing beyond the physical. But one cannot deny the great influence of Christianity in Western thinking, and I believe that one could detect the shadow of the dead god in many thinkers that believe they left all metaphysics behind. As the bones endure far longer than the living body, the structures that sustain metaphysical thinking endure well beyond metaphysical ideas. The distinction between the subjectivity of thought and the objectivity of bodies is one of these structures.

*Chapter One*

# On the Origin of the Difference
# of *Psyche* and *Soma* in Plato's *Timaeus*

P lato is commonly known in the history of philosophy as an initiator of a dualistic concept of body and soul that favors the soul at the expense of the body. By contrast, Nietzsche is known as the thinker who reversed the Platonic order between the "true" intelligible world and the "untrue" sensible world by reinscribing thinking in terms of intelligible ideas in a bodily activity. He is known as well as one who also attempted to think (in) the overcoming of the so-called platonic dualism.[1] Since then there have been many attempts to rethink what seems to be—for thought at least—an insurmountable gap between the sensible and the intelligible in terms of a more original unity. As I will show, in order to find this more original unity we do not need to "disprove" Plato, since Plato's text itself can be reread in a nondualistic manner. This requires that we focus less on *what* different voices in Plato's texts say and more on *how* thinking unfolds in the text. This chapter proposes especially a rereading of Plato's *Timaeus*, a text that deals with the creation of the cosmos and of human beings. But this text also deals—at another level—with the creation of a speech that attempts to articulate its own coming to be. This is why it lends itself particularly to question how we come to think the "body" that we find at play in our own thought.

Paul Friedländer points out that the *Timaeus* constitutes Plato's attempt to bring together the insights of the physicists concerning the nature of the physical world with the teleological principle of the idea of the good in such a way that the mechanical and accidental causes of the physical world are shown to be subordinated to the "good" as the highest principle of reason.[2] Almost all

commentaries on Plato's *Timaeus* have been faithful to this attempt by emphasizing the primacy of the supersensual eidetic principle in the becoming of
the world.[3]

The present reading of the *Timaeus*[4] distinguishes itself from traditional
interpretations insofar as the direction of its questioning is rather "nonpla-
tonic"—if we intend by "platonic" the maxim to let a discourse be guided by supersensual ideas or even a highest idea (goodness). I do not intend to set out
(like Friedländer and others) from the difference between physical causes and
eidetic cause and seek their unity by showing how the physical causes are subordinated to the eidetic cause. Rather, I will question *how* this distinction between a realm of the supersensual and the sensual *comes to be in and for thinking.*
This entails that in my reading I encounter the performativity of the text in its
coming to sense in a double sense—that is, in the genesis of what it has to say
and in the sensible traces that carry its meaning. In other words, my reading attempts to stay particularly sensible to the *way* what is thought and said arise in
thinking and saying. Thereby I seek to trace the genesis, that is, the original becoming of thinking and thus the becoming of a thinking that thinks (in) the
difference of body and "soul."

Like Nietzsche I will trace the distinction between a supersensual realm of
being and a sensual realm of being back to a "bodily" activity that withdraws from
conceptualization. The way I intend to explain the genesis of this difference also
draws from Heidegger's analysis of the origin of Greek (and Western) thought
through the differencing of thinking and being (*Scheidung von Sein und Denken*).
According to Heidegger, the differencing of being and thinking occurs when
thinking places itself over against being, conceiving being as permanent presence.
Consequently, the original occurrence of the disclosure of being in thinking and
the occurrence of the differencing of being and thinking conceals itself.

I will problematize with respect to Plato's *Timaeus* the relation between
the *soma* (body) and the psyche (soul) of the *kosmos* (world) and of humans by
tracing these notions back to the original occurrence of their differencing. This
differencing occurs in legein through *rhythm (rythmos)* and *harmony (harmo-
nia)*. Legein is commonly translated as saying or speaking. However, as we will
see, the way Plato uses this verb suggests that its more archaic senses reverber-
ate in it, namely the sense "to gather" and the sense "to count," or "to enumerate." Legein does not mean saying something that is already present to our
minds, but rather designates the occurrence through which first something
comes to appear as such and thus can be articulated. It is a differencing and
gathering that does not necessarily imply speech (words). Thus legein refers to
a broad sense of logos; it further points to an originary event of logos.[5] At the
very core of the legein through which things come to appear we will find what

Timaeus calls chora, a "place," previous to the legein, which may be conceived as an "abysmal ground" in which the differencing of psyche and soma, of eternal being and becoming, of the selfsame and the different, and thus of an intelligible and a sensible realm occur.

When we read the *Timaeus* we should be aware that Timaeus' discourse has mostly the character of a myth. In his middle and latest period, Plato speaks through myths when the possibility of a true logos, we might say of a rational conceptualization, reaches its limits.[6] When we try to give an account of the genesis of the world (as Plato's *Timaeus* does), we attempt to explain an occurrence that happened *before* there were human beings, and that means *before* the genesis of our own possibility of understanding and speaking. An attempt at any such genetic explanation necessarily has to cope with the limits of language and conceptualization. Plato copes with this limit by speaking through myths that consequently should not be taken as naive propositions of faith or as true propositions of some kind of "higher knowledge," but rather as images or signs that expose us to "what" cannot simply be conceptualized. Thus Timaeus calls his account a "likely story." A close reading of the *Timaeus* further reveals that Timaeus' mythical discourse on the creation of the world reflects the creation of his very speech; that is, it points to the origin and coming to be of thinking and speech. The parallel between the creation of the cosmos and Timaeus' speech does not necessarily indicate a "humanization" of the history of creation but may point to how the motion of thought mirrors the cosmos—that is, how thought arises with an understanding of the cosmos. Thereby the difficulty to articulate the beginning of the cosmos is reflected in how Timaeus repeatedly interrupts his discourse in order to begin again his speech with a different beginning.

## a.   The Broken Frame of Timaeus' Speech

Plato's *Timaeus* opens with a preliminary discourse that refers to a previous discussion on the ideal republic and is followed by Timaeus' speech, which treats the genesis of the world and of humans.[7] This speech is constituted by a preliminary remark and three parts in which Timaeus restarts his account on the genesis of the world from the beginning, and each time from a different beginning. In the first part, Timaeus talks about creation through nous ("thought")[8]; in the second part he talks about creation through necessity;[9] and in the third part he explains how nous and necessity work together in the creation of human beings.[10]

In his preliminary remarks, Timaeus draws a distinction between that which always is (*to on aei*) and has no becoming (*genesin ouk echon*) and that which is always becoming (*to gignomenon aei*) and therefore never is (*on oudepote*). *Being* is hereby conceived as *permanent presence* as distinguished from a becoming that has always already passed away and so is *not* anymore or is yet to become and so is *not* yet.[11] Whereas that which always is is apprehended through a noetic logos, that which is always becoming can only be conceived through the senses (*aisthesis*) by an opinion (*doxa*) without true logos. Since the cosmos, of which Timaeus will speak, is sensible and tangible and is always becoming, his speech, as he says, will belong to the order of doxa.

According to Timaeus mythical discourse, the cosmos has an origin and a maker (the *demiourgos*) who created it by looking at what is eternal (*aidios*). Further it was created as a copy (*eikon*) of the original image that is apprehensible by logos and nous ("thought") and which is eternally selfsame. Thus, Timaeus at first envisions the cosmos under the perspective of *techne*, as being created similar to the manner in which a cabinetmaker would make a table—having the image of a table in mind according to which the table is made. This will allow him to apprehend the creation of the cosmos through logos and make his speech, which belongs to the order of doxa, at least probable, even if it cannot be known to be true. And yet this relation between original model and image, which is the framework within which the creation of the cosmos takes place, will be problematized and interrupted by what will be called chora, a "place" of becoming that essentially escapes noetic logos (logos insofar as it follows reason). With respect to Timaeus' speech we may say that his speaking, his logos, moves within the "spacing" of eternal image and mutable copy, between that which always is and that which always changes and therefore never is. This occurs in such a way as to bring forth in his words this difference for the listener/reader. But his speech will be continually interrupted and displaced in such a way as to prevent a properly ordered speech according to the scheme "original model and copy." Indeed, it will be interrupted and displaced at its very beginning. The issue (and failure) of a proper beginning under the direction of nous and logos will be continually reinitiated because interruption and displacement occur at the very beginning of the creation of the cosmos and correspondingly at the beginning of the creation of Timaeus' speech.

## b.   The Demiurge and the "Nurse of all Becoming"

In the creation of the cosmos, Timaeus distinguishes two kinds of causes, the necessary and the divine.[12] The necessary cause refers to physical laws of nature.[13] It is said to be inferior to the divine cause (the demiurge), insofar as the divine maker of the cosmos tends to conduct also that which is becoming through necessity to the best end[14] by creating everything, as far as possible, in his own likeness.[15] In accordance with this priority, Timaeus will attempt in his discourse to subordinate the necessary and accidental causes to the primary divine cause.

However, the divine maker is not the only cause of the cosmos. He did not create the cosmos from nothing (like a cabinetmaker does not create the material from which he makes a table, and like Timaeus does not create his speech from nothing). According to Timaeus, already before the creation of the cosmos there was something visible and therefore corporeal (*somaton*) that was in a state of motion, although in a discordant (*plemmelos*) and disorderly (*ataktos*) motion.[16] The adverb *plemmelos* is formed by "*plen*" and "*melos*" and means literally "against the melody"—that is, discordant and inharmonious. In the creation of the world, the demiurge "took over all that was visible" and brought it into order out of disorder.[17] In other words, he brought what was moving disharmoniously and without order into a harmoniously ordered rhythmic movement.

Timaeus will speak more explicitly of this primordial disordered visible that was there already before the creation in the second part of his discourse. Thereby he will find himself forced to introduce, besides the model and the copy, a third and somewhat difficult and obscure form (*eidos*), a force (*dunamis*) that he calls "the receptacle, and as it were the nurse, of all becoming"[18] Whereas the model is that *from which* something is copied, and the copy is that which becomes, the nurse of all becoming is that *in which* something becomes.[19] She "is an invisible and formless being which receives all things and in some mysterious way partakes of the intelligible, and is most incomprehensible."[20] Even though she is invisible herself, the nurse of all becoming is that in which the visible is formed, she is the "space" (chora) of becoming. Timaeus describes her as a "moulding-stuff" (*ekmageion*) that is moved and marked by that which enters it, appearing differently at different times.[21] So the part of her that is being set on fire appears as fire, her liquid part appears as water, earth, and air.[22]

The "nurse of all becoming" was there already before the maker of the cosmos began to form; that is, before he began to order the visible in her according to his own image. There were somehow "traces" of fire, earth, water, and air already there in the space of becoming, even though one cannot properly name them as such[23] because fire, earth, water, and air were created later according to (and for) a logos by the maker of the cosmos. There was nothing intelligible before the creation; there were no names. (24) And yet Timaeus speaks of "something" corporeal (not a body or thing one could name) that shook the "nurse of the becoming" who, in her turn, being completely out of balance, shook the "not-yet-elements." She thereby functioned like a winnowing machine, scattering away from one another the "not-yet-elements" that were most unlike and pressing those together that were most similar, but her motion was without any measure or proportion[25] and the scattering and collecting were completely accidental.

The chora, which was there before any creation according to a noetic logos, is more primordial than the distinction between the eternal selfsame and becoming, between original image and copy. She is more primordial than the distinction between the intelligible and the sensible, because this distinction presupposes a noetic logos. We cannot properly think her because she is more primordial than this noetic logos.[26] She is something like (but not properly) an invisible, formless accidentally moving "space" *in* which creation through nous occurs. She is a space that composes no solid visible or intelligible ground: an abysmal ground in which, when we try to think her, our concepts of logos and soma fail.[27]

Seeking the origin of the creation, Timaeus thus hits "something" that is more primordial than the logos according to which he attempts to order his speech: a "ground" in which his speech (logos) arises and which simultaneously withdraws from his speech. Chora is not only the abysmal ground in which visible things are created through logos by the maker of the universe, but it is also the abysmal ground in which Timaeus' (Plato's) and our own visible (written) and audible (spoken) intelligible words come to be. In fact, the chora, as Timaeus describes it, echoes the not yet ordered bodily motions and resistances that we find at play as we attempt to conceptualize a new thought.

### c.   The Creation of the Psyche of the Cosmos

In his first speech, Timaeus gives the following account on the creation of the cosmos: In order to be created according to the image of its creator, the cosmos had to have nous ("thought"), which presupposes a psyche.[28] Plato calls psyche a self-moving principle of movement[29] and that through which a body lives—that is, a "life-force."[30] The cosmos is itself a living being insofar as it has a psyche.

Despite his claim that she was made prior to the body, Timaeus speaks of the psyche only after his account of the creation of the body of the cosmos. At first his speech holds on to the visible, whose becoming he attempts to trace back to a primordial nous. Like the creator, he takes over the visible and attempts to put it into order.

According to Timaeus, when the demiurge created the body of the cosmos he used *all* the elements (leaving nothing visible out of order) and put them into determinate proportions. He thereby made *one* whole living being in the shape of a circle, leaving *nothing* outside it. It was given a circular movement, the movement of the same, which belongs mostly to nous.[31] It seems, then, that the chora as she was before the creation has disappeared—and yet, in his first speech, Timaeus still has not spoken of her. The initially disappeared chora is still to appear.

The psyche was placed in the middle of the body of the cosmos expanding all through it and covering the body from the outside. She was made in the following manner:

> Midway between the Being [ousia] which is indivisible and remains always the same and the Being which is transient and divisible in bodies, He [the creator] blended a third form [eidos] of Being compounded out of the twain, that is to say, out of Same and the Other [athaterou the Different]; and in like manner He compounded it midway between that one of them which is indivisible and that one which is divisible in bodies. And He took the three of them, and blend them all together into one form, by forcing the Other [Different] into union with the Same, in spite of its being naturally difficult to mix.[32]

The composition of the psyche out of what at first just seem abstract terms becomes more understandable if we take into account its Pythagorean background and the legein—that is, the "saying" in which things come to appear. Taylor points out with reference to Aristotle's interpretation of this passage, that the "Same" and the "Different" for Plato are the Pythagorean *stoicheia* (principles or primordial elements) which are also the stoicheia of the objects that the psyche knows.[33] This means that the primordial elements of the psyche are also the primordial elements of what she comes to "know" through legein. A key to understand why Timaeus describes the composition of the psyche as a mixture and harmony of the same and the different is her "perceptive activity" (in the sense of legein). For Plato, as for the Pythagoreans, "like knows like." That means that the psyche must be like the objects she knows. Objects, as will be explained later, are known with respect to their being same or different. And the psyche can tell (legein) and thus recognize something with respect to its being different or same only insofar as she is both (different and same) herself.

We will have difficulties in understanding how the psyche can "be" same and different and how objects are known to be same or different as long as we think of the psyche as a perceiving (or thinking) substance over against perceived objects. But if we consider that the psyche and "what" is known are originally disclosed as such only *in* the occurrence of a legein, we may rather attempt to think the psyche and the things she comes to know *through* the disclosive legein—that is, in questioning originally the coming to be of legein. In other words, if we follow attentively how perceiving or thinking of the same and different comes to be, legein comes first, and out of the occurrence of legein the concepts of psyche and of what is perceived according to the same and the different emerge.

But before turning our attention to the legein of the psyche, I would like to point at the fact that, according to Timaeus' description, the psyche unites in *one form* components that are "naturally difficult to mix [*dusmeikton*]"—that is, the same and the different, the unchangeable and the mutable, what pertains to the order of logos and what pertains to the body. We could say, then, that the one form of the psyche in herself harmoniously unites difference. Harmony, in Greek thought, means the bringing together of opposites, of what is "hostile" to each other (*sunthesin enantion*).[34] Like in a musical harmony (and the Pythagorean sense of harmony which is at play in the *Timaeus* is thought with reference to music), the unity of these opposites does not dissolve the single character of what is united. With the solution of the opposites harmony itself would be dissolved. Similarly in the composition and in the "perception" (legein) of the psyche sameness and difference are thought of as being united *as such* without being dissolved in a homogenous unity.

To understand the psyche's "perception" or "knowledge" of the cosmos, one needs to take into account the movement (*kinesis*) of the psyche. According to Timaeus, the creator divided the psyche into portions. These portions, Timaeus continues, correspond to a mathematical formula that gives the intervals of a melodic progression.[35] We see how, again, harmony plays a central role in the creation of the psyche. The portions, Timaeus continues, were then split into two strands that were united in order to form two opposite circular movements, the outer, *sovereign movement* pertaining to the nature of the *same* and the inner movement pertaining to the nature of the different. Again, in the architecture of the cosmos, the same (and thus logos) is said to prevail over the different.[36] The inner circle was split again into seven different circles that would constitute the orbits of the seven planets.[37] The planets, moved by the cycles of the psyche, will preserve countable time through the rhythm of night and day, of the course of the moon and of the different planets as they move together.[38]

The harmony of the psyche of the cosmos appears now in the different circular movements through which she appropriates knowledge of herself as well as of the visible bodies. The psyche acquires knowledge of something, says Timaeus, by getting in touch with it (*ephaptetai*) and by moving throughout her whole being. Since she is herself harmoniously the same and the different, the indivisible and the divisible belonging to bodies, she is able, he says, to announce to herself (*legei*) what the touched thing is and how it is, both in the sphere of the becoming and in that of the selfsame. Moving in a circular motion throughout herself, she bends back, reflects on herself, and is thereby able to tell herself whether the touched thing is selfidentical or changeable, indivisible or divisible, and what relation it has with other things in time and space.[39]

So much for Timaeus' explicit account of how the psyche gains knowledge. However, beyond this explicit account, a few questions remain open. Timaeus claims that the psyche of the cosmos gains knowledge of that which belongs to the order of the *selfsame* insofar as she is herself constituted in part by the indivisible and selfsame. But the psyche is, by definition, a selfmoving "force," and movement, as Timaeus will say, takes place only where difference reigns.[40] If she is able to recognize the "Same," there must be, then, *in* her motion, *in* the reigning of difference, something escaping this motion, something selfsame that escapes time, maybe a moment of "eternal" (in the sense of timeless) suspense inherent to her rhythmic and harmonious cyclical motions. We can think this moment of suspense when we are attentive, for instance, to the ungraspable moment in which in our breathing inhaling turns to exhaling and vice versa. There is a moment where we are neither inhaling nor exhaling. One may also think of a swing that, when swinging up at a certain point, reaches its peak and remains suspended for a moment before swinging down again. Within Plato's *Timaeus* there is evidence of a similar moment if we think of the circle of the planets which periodically converge to a same constellation if we measure them, as Timaeus says, with the circle of the same[41]—that is, with the stars that appear to remain in the same position.[42] The psyche of the cosmos can recognize that which belongs to the order of the unchangeable selfsame only in a timeless moment of suspended motion within her cyclical motion.

With this interpretation I am going beyond what Timaeus explicitly says. Here, as in the following paragraphs, I intend to explicate further than Timaeus does the occurrence of the legein *from within* this occurrence. I shall not consider the legein as an occurrence that I objectify by representing Timaeus' description in my mind as something that occurs independently from my thinking. Rather I will consider the legein as a coming to be also of my own thinking and I will attempt to retrace the sensible movements at play in its coming to be from its very beginning.

The legein is initiated, Timaeus says, "whenever the psyche gets in touch with something."[43] The word "touching" (ephaptetai) appears in the middle form, which is neither active nor passive. That means that touching, at the outset, is thought of without primary agent, so that we might just say: touching occurs. Prior to the touching, nothing is recognized; that is, nothing is disclosed for a perception as such. The touch at first is blind.[44] Now, if we try to think *within* the occurrence of the legein and of the touch, if we think *in* the disclosing of something through the legein, we may say that, from out of a blind touching, a differencing of the same and the other occurs, so that "something" appears as such and as being different or selfsame.

On the one hand, the appearance or disclosure of something *eternally selfsame* occurs within the movement of the psyche in a differencing (suspension) from motion and change. On the other hand, the disclosure of something *divisible and becoming* (i.e., the disclosure of visible bodies) occurs as a differencing from the eternally self-same. The visible is disclosed in its becoming (*as* that which is *not* selfsame but is coming to be or passing away) only by differing from the moment of timeless suspense within what Timaeus describes as the cyclical motions of the psyche. Visible bodies are recognized in their becoming only insofar they are not yet or not anymore with respect to what I called a moment of suspension within the becoming. Recall Timaeus' preliminary remarks in which he says that that which is always becoming (visible bodies) never is.[45] The visible is disclosed in its becoming (in its not-being) in the occurrence of its differencing from the eternally selfsame (which always is).

An example may make this clearer: When we recognize a visible body—for instance, a flower—the notion of the flower belongs to the order of the self-same. But to know that the visible thing we call flower belongs to the order of the divisible and changing implies that in its singularity and mutability (in its becoming) it differs from the notion flower. The visible thing *as* becoming withdraws from "its" notion (idea) and can be recognized as becoming only in a differing (departing) from the selfsame (from what in a Platonic sense *is*). The sense of this differing, of this withdrawing from what *is* (permanently present) allows us to recognize a visible tangible body *in its becoming*.

Any notion we have (may it be of something invisible or visible) is already the result of a legein understood as an originating occurrence of a differencing of same and other. Now, this also implies that the notion psyche (as well as the notion *soma*, body) is the result, a "product"[46] of a legein. In our common thinking, we do not thematize and are not aware of this originating dimension of thinking, because this dimension withdraws from conceptualization and cannot be intended like an object. It remains thinking's hidden source. Timaeus points at this hidden source when he describes through a myth the constitution (creation) of the psyche and her activity in a legein. If we take his descriptions straightforwardly, what he says would simply be an odd tale. My claim is that a key to understanding what this mythical narration is pointing to can be found in the occurrence of the legein, because through a legein something at first is disclosed in perception and thought. To think the legein originally without presupposing what is disclosed through it (concepts and propositions) is a difficult task. It requires that we try to "think" the movement of a differencing without presupposing neither agent (a subject) nor object since, when we think the legein as a differencing that is an activity of a subject, we already have lost the original dimension of the legein. At the source of the legein there is no (recognizable) subject or agent nor a (recognizable object), but just the originating movement of a differencing. This way of thinking takes of course a different view on the genesis of thinking with respect to the tale of a cosmic demiurge. In my interpretation, the cosmic demiurge is a reflection of the "making" of

Timaeus' speech and at the same time a model that allows Timaeus to order his speech. In my analysis of the legein I attempt to describe more originally the coming to be of order out of disorder; "more originally" in this case means: without presupposing an already given order.[47] The problem here of course is, how to think this originating movement, since it cannot be grasped by conceptualization? We may get closer to an answer through what follows.

### d.   Human *Legein*

An attempt to think the cosmic legein within its occurrence presupposes that this occurrence can be experienced and that there can be an awareness of it (even though it withdraws from proper articulation). Indeed, there is enough evidence in the *Timaeus* that the human legein does not differ essentially from the cosmic legein, even though the human psyche is, in Timaeus' narration, farther away from the eternal model than the cosmic psyche. According to Timaeus, humans were created partly in a *second degree* of imitation: on the one hand they have an immortal psyche that was created by the maker of the universe, but on the other hand they have a mortal psyche[48] and mortal bodies that were created by gods who, in their turn, had been created by the original creator.[49]

As Timaeus states toward the end of his first speech, the creator mixed the immortal *psuchai* that would belong to humans "somewhat in the same manner" as he mixed the soul of the universe, but second or third in degree of purity.[50] The creator then ordered the gods he had created to take over the immortal psyche and to create the human body according to the laws imposed by him. Thus, according to his order, human bodies were subject to influx and efflux that at first appeared as a mighty river in which the courses of the psyche violently rolled along without order or rhythm (*ataktos*) and without logos in all six kinds of motion (up, down, front, back, right, left).

This description of the initial state of creation strikingly resembles the one of the chora that before the creation was said to move without the ordering of a logos that follows noetic knowledge and without rhythm. Indeed, the creation of humans mirrors the one of the cosmos. Even though Timaeus says that the maker of the universe had ordered *all* the visible bodies through logos, making *one* living being out of it, chora reappears in a second generation as the "abysmal," accidentally moving ground out of which creation through logos occurs.

The mighty river by which humans were flooded at the beginning of the creation was caused by the "flood which supplied the food" and even more by "sensations" (aistheseis).[51] Sensations occurred as the result of colliding bodies (and not of harmonious touch). When a body from the outside collided with the human body, its motions would be carried through the body to the psyche, causing disordered motions. In the beginning, the sensations were so strong, Timaeus says, that they totally blocked the course of the same by their opposing current.[52] Likewise, the courses of the different were scattered in all their proportions, causing all sorts of fractures and disruptions, so that the courses of the different would move completely without logos.[53] This initial state of overpowering disorder is slowly brought into order, as the impulse of growth and the flood of nourishment get weaker.[54]

After this dramatic account of the initial state of human creation, Timaeus starts to give a "more exact exposition"[55] of the creation of humans. He attempts to pursue his speech in a more organized way, describing how order came into the motions of the human psyche.[56] One of the first things the gods created after they bound the immortal soul in the head was the eyes. The eyes are the main organ that will allow humans to order the courses of their psuchai. A passage in which Timaeus describes how sight occurs helps us to understand more precisely how the psyche perceives and comes to know through legein visible and tangible bodies and thus how visible and tangible bodies are connected with the psyche and her faculty of understanding. Through the eyes, says Timaeus, fire flows similar to the fire of daylight.

> When the light of day surrounds the stream of vision, the like falls upon like, and they coalesce, and one body is formed by natural affinity in the line of vision, wherever the light that falls from within meets with an external object. And the whole stream of vision, being similarly affected in virtue of similarity, diffuses motions of what it touches or what touches it over the whole body, until they reach the soul, causing that perception which we call sight.[57]

In sight, the fire of the eyes, the fire of daylight and the fire of that which is seen converge.[58] The stream of vision touches the fire of the things, which, insofar as it is made of the same element, transmits its motion to the stream of vision. The motion of that which is seen is transmitted through the *whole* body to the course of the psyche and is thus perceived.

The touch and the motion through which something is seen at first seems to have a physical nature: particles encounter particles, initiating a movement that pervades, as Timaeus says, the whole body and which is transmitted to the motions of the psyche. Thus, there seems to be an unbroken continuity between the motion of the body and the motion of the psyche. Where and how exactly the transition from the motion of the one to the other happens, remains unclear. It seems to be only a question of order or of the direction that might be given either by nous or by necessity (or by chora). But Timaeus ultimately fails to give a proper account of where the boundary between psyche and soma is to

be drawn, which makes the difference between the two very questionable.
Viewed from within the occurrence—that is, the movement of legein (in the
differencing of same and other)— however, it makes perfect sense that a distinction between psyche and soma cannot be made, insofar as in the occurrence
of their differencing they are not yet differentiated. Psyche and soma, understood as two different concepts are the result of a differencing. Where they
appear in separate terms, they are not thought of as in movement anymore but
with reference to permanent (abstract) ideas. The way they *actually occur* in the
genesis of thinking withdraws from conceptualizing thought. It might be interesting to remind us, at this point, that in Homer soma means the dead body,
the body without life, and that psyche designates what leaves the body at its
death.[59] The terms "soma" and "psyche" acquire their meaning when life and
movement cease. Likewise we conceive them through distinct terms only when
we loose touch in our thinking with the original occurrence (life) in which
beings and thinking are disclosed—that is, when the original dimension of life
withdraws. This suggests that legein not only differentiates but originarily also
gathers the sense of psyche and soma. Legein occurs as a bodily activity.

Seeing is described by Timaeus similarly to the legein of the psyche of
the cosmos. Insofar as the human psyche is made like the psyche of the cosmos
(even though inferior in purity), we may try to join the two descriptions in
order to get a fuller account of the legein in which humans participate. We
should be aware, however, that human seeing is described with reference to visible and tangible bodies (and not with reference to invisible ideas).

Let us first describe the legein from a point of view from which Timaeus
might envision it (i.e., not from within the legein): The converging of the fire
of the stream of vision, of what is seen and of daylight, is a touching which initiates a particular legein. Through this touch, the motion of what is touched
permeates our whole psychophysical being. Now, in order to see and discern
what is seen *as such*—that is, what it is and how it is in its relation to other
things in time and space—the selfsame must be distinguished from the different. As thought from *within* the very origin of the occurrence of legein (or
seeing), the stream of vision, the daylight, and what is touched are clearly distinguished only *after* the legein is completed. The process of seeing, the coming
to see, is, at its source, blind, although it involves motions of which one might
have awareness. The differencing involved in the legein occurs (recall what was
said with respect to the cosmic psyche) in a moment of suspension of the passing away in the process of becoming. We might say that the motions of legein
*gather* in this moment of suspension.[60]

Two passages from different dialogues of Plato point to the gathering in
perception and thought. These passages will also allow us to further develop a

thinking of the occurrence of legein. In the *Phaedrus* Socrates says: "For a human being must understand according to *eidos* what is said, going from many perceptions (*aistheseon*) to a one gathered together by reckoning (*logismo*)."[61]

For Plato, eidos is the selfsame unchangeable "form" through which something is thought as such.[62] It is described here as emerging from many perceptions, or, we may say, from blind impressions enacted through touching. The eidos is one. This "one" emerges in a gathering from impressions that undergo a process of differencing of selfsame and different. The one emerges in the differencing as a suspension from motion and passing away.

A passage from Plato's *Phaedo* will allow us to think more fully another aspect of the legein, namely the differentiation of body and psyche it implies. The psyche, Socrates says there, needs to be purified (*katharsis*) through her separation (*chorizein*) from the body. This "separation" consists in making the psyche get used to collect herself (*sunageiresthai*—note the middle form of the verb)[63] from all directions out of the body and "to gather herself (*athroizesthai*) and to persist, as far as possible, for herself now and later, freed as from chains from the body."[64]

I put the word "separation" in quotation marks to indicate that the separation of psyche and soma Socrates speaks of does not end in an absolute separation. The process of separation remains uncompleted. The psyche can persist for herself only "as far as possible."[65] As long as we live, our psyche will never be completely separated from the body. It would be more appropriate, therefore, to speak of a differencing of psyche and soma through a legein—that is, a gathering in one eidos. Soma thereby emerges as that from which a differencing occurs. "From" in the sense of "getting away from" the blind unordered manifold sensual impressions, but "from" also in the sense of the original abysmal ground, the chora. Psyche, in turn, emerges as that to which the differencing leads. She is not simply the agent of the legein. In this context it is important to stress that the verbs "sunageiresthai" (collect) and "athroizesthai" (gather) appear in their middle form. That means that the occurrence of gathering is neither active nor passive, it has no agent and no object, but is thought from within its occurrence.

## e.   The Genesis of Sameness in an Eternal Return

But why does a gathering into one eidos occur? How can we think in unities if the source of our understanding appears to be manifold? Plato's answer to this question is well known: unchangeable unities, *forms* (*eide*) must be there before a particular occurrence of a perception.[66] In the *Phaedo* Socrates says that we conceive the ideas through which we understand something as such before our birth and that we remember them in our lives. The source of the ideas is said to be outside the mortal legein, as also the chora was there before creation through a logos. And yet, as long as we live, ideas are disclosed for us only in a *noein* occurring through a legein. There are no forms for themselves written in the heavens independently of a perception.

But from where, then, do we get a sense of the "one"?[67] How can we think sameness within the realm of becoming? This issue was addressed earlier but needs further elaboration. In the motion of the psyche, so was argued, there must be something that escapes this motion, a moment of timeless suspense, an interruption of time within time. According to Timaeus, the planets were created as the organs of time. Time comes to be through the cyclical motions of the planets, through the alternation of night and day and the cycle of the moon and the other planets.[68] The sameness or eternity of the creator is imitated, as Timaeus says, through the rhythmical ("eternal") return of all planets to an original constellation:

> It is still quite possible to perceive that the complete number of Time fulfills the Complete Year when all the eight circuits [of the eight planets], with their relative speeds, finish together and come to a head, when measured by the revolution of the Same and Similarly-moving. In this wise and for these reasons were generated all those stars which turn themselves about as they travel through Heaven, to the end that this universe might be as similar as possible to the perfect and intelligible Living Creature in respect of its imitation of the Eternal Nature thereof.[69]

The complete year Timaeus speaks of is the Great World-Year, which is completed when all the planets return simultaneously to a same constellation. Even though nobody can possibly be witness to such a year in her/his lifetime, we can experience a rhythmical return on a smaller scale in the regular courses of the sun and the moon and the other star constellations. Time is countable in the rhythmic return of specific constellations to relative positions. In order to count time, we need to divide it into unities—that is, into "ones." These "ones" are constituted in the rhythmic return of a movement to a specific constellation of bodies (for example, each time the sun sets one day passes). It is in this rhythmic return that we get a sense of "eternity" within movement.

In fact, Timaeus says that seeing the movement of the stars (the cosmic psyche) allows humans to order the courses of their own motions.[70] Thus, human legein is dependent upon the cosmic legein and we owe our capacity to think permanent unities to the cyclical motions of the stars. The very moment of return, the "now," has been problematized throughout our philosophical tradition. When we try to grasp it objectively, it has already passed away. And yet we can take a phenomenological approach in trying to think within the experience of the occurrence of a legein; that is, to think time not objectively over against us but through our experience of time.[71] Then a possibility opens up for thinking in the (re)tension of the not yet and no longer, to expand, as it were, the rhythmical beat of time in the suspense of its passing away. So, the legein, the differencing of same and different, of body and psyche, can be understood as occurring in the gathering of our motions, in the retention of the passing away and in the suspense of the coming to be that is connected to the rhythm of celestial bodies.

## f.  Conclusion

The occurrence of gathering and differencing (legein) in which the concepts soma and psyche arise cannot be said to pertain either to the order of the intelligible or of the sensible because in Plato these terms acquire their meaning in their opposition. The source of the legein, the chora, remains abysmal insofar as it withdraws from the noetic logos. This means that the Platonic concepts of psyche and soma are products of an occurrence that, at its source, escapes language and conceptuality.

Even thought the concept of soma (body) arises only as a result of legein, as we saw, legein is a process of coming to perceive and think of things, which occurs through bodily motions. At the same time, for Plato legein is an activity of psyche. Thus, the place where one finds the lived body in thinking in Plato is psyche. Although Plato claims that part of psyche belongs to the order of the selfsame and that he tends to associate psyche with the order of the selfsame, still psyche occurs in motions that differentiate and gather at once and it therefore belongs (also) to the order of becoming that is apprehended through the senses. Furthermore, the differencing and gathering that allows us to understand things as such is regulated through the cyclic motions of celestial bodies. In order to be regulated by them, the human psyche needs to see them, which occurs also through the body. The interpretation of psyche as a bodily occurrence is suggested as well by the fact that Timaeus is not able to distinguish clearly the motions of the body from the motions of the psyche. In the light of this inability it makes sense that Aristotle will conceive psyche as nothing but the activity of a living body.

But Plato himself did not determine psyche this way and—on the contrary, as it appears—always took care to differentiate psyche from the body. A main reason for this is certainly ethical. If we think back at Timaeus' account of how human beings were overwhelmed, at the beginning of their creation, by violent, disruptive motions, we may get a sense of how Plato felt a necessity for bringing rhythm and harmony into the different struggling motions inherent in human beings. To differentiate the selfsame from becoming by conceiving the eternal selfsame as the transcendent cause (ground) and telos of the sensible world would allow the establishment of a measure by means of which thinking could gain a stability and order in the midst of the ever changing overwhelming nature in its becoming (*phusis*). Today, our urge appears different, in the sense that we are trained to gather our thoughts into conceptualities, so much so that we easily lose touch with the bodily differencing-gathering itself in which language and thought come to be. Thus, our ethical concern today almost appears as reversal of Plato's concern; namely to revive the lived grounds in which thought arises, as opaque and difficult to grasp as they may appear.

*Chapter Two*

# The Return of the Body in Exile
## Nietzsche

Plato's *Timaeus* allows us to consider the emerging of a differentiation between the sensible and the intelligible in thought and an originary bodily dimension in thought from which this difference arises. These considerations put into question the difference between the sensible and the intelligible. At the same time, the originary bodily dimension in thought is constantly obscured by the very difference between the sensible and the intelligible—and accordingly between body and mind—that it allows to emerge. Thus, Plato's *Timaeus* presents us with a limit with respect to the possibility of thinking the bodily dimension in thought. This is a limit in a twofold sense, since it delineates both the arising of thought as a bodily event and the loss of this event in the differentiation of the sensible and the intelligible.[1]

Nietzsche's thought challenges us with another limit, one that appears to be closer to contemporary thinkers. At this limit the difference between body and thinking presents itself as a clear and distinct "object" of thought that appears to leave no room for something outside itself. And yet, at this limit a threshold opens to a reconsideration of the bodily dimension in thought. Nineteen centuries of Western history separate Nietzsche's philosophy from Plato's, a history with multiple lineages, which includes among its most influential events the arising of Christianity in the Middle Ages and the opening of the era of modern science in the seventeenth century. In different and multiple ways both events sharpen a dualism between mind and body or between a spiritual world and a material world that germinated in Plato's thought and that, after having undergone various shifts and transformations, informs Nietzsche's life and thought and his passionate battle to overthrow the metaphysical dualism in a reevaluation of values.

At the beginning of modern philosophy the question of the body shifts away from its connection with the soul and comes to stand in an opposition to thought, while the question of the soul is replaced by the exploration of human consciousness. One can see this occurring in Descartes' second Meditation, when he reconsiders what in Scholasticism is conceived to be attributes of the soul—namely nutrition, movement, sense-perception, and thought—and when he rearranges nutrition, movement, and sense-perception under what belongs to the body (and may be doubted) and opposes these to thinking, so that in the end thinking is the only attribute that truly belongs to the "I."[2]

With the disappearing of the soul the lived body is exiled. It has no place in consciousness, since the feelings and bodily motions of which I am conscious become thought contents that are immaterial and therefore distinct from bodies. The lived body has no place in the material world either, since bodies in the world are accessed objectively as that which can be scientifically (quantitatively) measured. Basically, bodies are not different from corpses. This is where Nietzsche enters the scene as an advocate for the exiled body. Nietzsche has been repeatedly celebrated as the philosopher who, after centuries of repression of the body for the sake of the primacy of reason, placed again our bodily reality at the center of philosophic reflection. He thereby simply seems to reverse the metaphysical relation between sensibility and reason. Whereas traditional metaphysical thinkers regard the intelligible ideas as highest values that give a permanent sense to life, Nietzsche regards them as products of an always changing, groundless sensible life. He regards them as fictions that have the function to grant to human beings the illusion of some kind of consistency in life.

However, this reversal of a metaphysical dualism between a true intelligible world and an apparent sensible world is not as simple as it may, at first, appear; not only because a simple reversal of the metaphysical dualism would still affirm the dualism but also because this dualism is not a logical construct one may wipe out at will, since it is rooted in values and thus in a lived reality that shapes living bodies.

Nietzsche is well aware of that. As I will show, Nietzsche not only incorporates the Christian tradition but also Kantian thought in his belief that anything we think belongs to the realm of consciousness and consequently is mere appearance. Yet, Nietzsche also begins to break these lineages he incorporates in what Heidegger calls a "twisting free" (*Herausdrehung*) of Platonism; that is, an overcoming of the metaphysical opposition between reason and sensibility, between true and seeming world.[3]

A famous passage in Nietzsche's "Twilight of the Idols" most poignantly announces this twisting free of what Nietzsche calls a "history of error." This is the well-known final passage in a short section titled "How the 'True World' Became a Fable," which ends in the following way

> The true world—we have abolished. What world has remained? The apparent one perhaps? But no! With the true world we have also abolished the apparent one.[4]

This little passage has been often discussed and for good reasons; it indicates a threshold for contemporary thought. It announces the breakdown of a binary structure that has organized Western philosophy and the understanding and valorization of a certain world order. One may go along with Heidegger and understand this threshold as the beginning of the end of history or one may go along with contemporary thinkers like Derrida and Nancy in France and Sallis and Scott in the United States (to name only a few) who would rather understand this as a beginning of new possibilities of thought. In any case, the moment of the "twisting free" from the fable of the two worlds calls for ways of thinking that are radically different from traditional thought. In these different ways of thinking the enactment of thinking plays a more prominent role than that which is thought. Not the "what" but the "how" of thinking becomes decisive. In this turn to the performative aspect of thinking also appears what I call the bodily dimension of Nietzsche's thought.

The return to the exiled body in Nietzsche's thought is not simply a happy homecoming. In a certain way the body that returns remains in exile. The body violently irrupts orders of thought that do not readily give way to the ancient intruder, which leads to a strange contradictory and yet productive coexistence. The following discussion follows the path that leads from the exclusion of the lived body in a Kantian frame of mind—that is, in a way of thinking that objectifies what it thinks and treats the body like a mere appearance (the appearance of a corpse that is detached from consciousness)—to the reemerging of the lived body in the performativity of Nietzsche's thought and writing. This path is tied to the history of Platonism in which a two-world order is formed according to which truth and being are not to be found in the sensible world and the body but in a world beyond, the intelligible world of ideas. I therefore will briefly reconsider what in "Twilight of the Idols" Nietzsche calls the "history of an error," highlighting only a few points from "How the 'True World' Became a Fable," which I consider relevant for the present discussion. We will see that Nietzsche's thought does not simply begin once the true world has become a fable but that it incorporates this history of an error, repeating it to a certain extent, so that the way Nietzsche thinks the body is tied to this history.

### a.   Overturning Platonism

According to Nietzsche, it is only with Platonism—that is, in the way Christian belief reshapes Plato's thought, that—the "history of an error" properly begins. With Plato the true world still remains "relatively sensible," which means that the two worlds did not yet split. Plato incorporated the idea of the true world; that is, ideas are part of the sensible world. But under the influence of Christianity the Platonic thought that only the unchangeable "ideas" (the forms or shapes of the good, of the beautiful, of truth, etc.) truly are, whereas the things we perceive through the senses in truth are not, this thought develops in such a way that the unchangeable forms become attributes of God and of a world to come, a world that remains unattainable for humans as long as they live. This faith in a perfect world to come constitutes a sense of life in the most profound way. It allows humans to turn away from the sufferings, injustices, and mortality of life and to hope for a better future after death.[5]

Yet according to traditional metaphysics, not only goodness, truth, and perfection are attributes of God, but this is also the case for the principles of reason of which we have immediate insight. These principles include the law of identity, the law of the contradiction, and the principle of sufficient reason (Leibniz' *principium reddaendae rationis sufficientis*). The a priori principles of reason are understood to be outside of the order of time, like the kingdom of God, and they are understood to be as much constitutive of our faculty of cognition as his goodness, truth, and perfection. This means that they are not just abstract principles for the employment of understanding but that they imply a most intimate feeling of sense and truth. They are *values* for human existence.

With the era of enlightenment arises the idea that truth should be obtained not primarily through faith but through reason, and reason cannot proof a world beyond our earthly world. But even if, then, the belief in a kingdom of God becomes questionable, still the intimate feeling of certitude, the belief in the truth of a priori principles, endures. Exemplary in this respect is, for Nietzsche, the philosophy of Kant as Schopenhauer taught it to Nietzsche. As Nietzsche sees it, in Kant's principles of reason still lives the shadow of the dead God. Even though in his *Critique of Pure Reason* Kant maintains that we cannot have any knowledge of metaphysical ideas, reason imposes us to assume certain metaphysical principles, like freedom and God, since these alone allow us to live a life that has moral worth. Thus, the true world becomes a moral imperative, even though we can have no knowledge of it.[6]

The "fable of the true world," as Nietzsche recounts it, continues with the emergence of positivism, which radicalizes the rational position in the claim that what we don't know we cannot assume. Consequently, the true world disappears.[7]

In *The Will to Power* Nietzsche describes this occurrence as the devaluation of the highest values. It marks a form of nihilism.[8] By affirming this nihilism,[9] by actively abolishing the true world, the final stage of the fable is reached where not only the true world but with it the apparent one disappears.[10]

The story of how the "true world" became a fable crystallizes the way Nietzsche situates his own thought in Western history. It also brings forth the limit of Nietzsche's thought. One can see how Nietzsche performs an active nihilism in his writings when he declares that what appears as truths are mere fictions. Less clear is what happens in the last stage of the fable. What happens once we have abolished both worlds, the true intelligible world and the apparent sensible world? How are we to understand thought and ideas as well as the body once the paradigm that made both intelligible and meaningful disappears? "Incipit Zarathustra," Nietzsche writes, however Zarathustra is only a prophet of a world to come.

I believe that part of what hinders Nietzsche's thought from passing the threshold that is marked by the disappearing of the "two-world order" is his Kantian inheritance. In *The Critique of Pure Reason*, the principles of understanding (the categories of quantity, quality, relation, and modality) are constitutive for the world as it appears to us. They prescribe laws to nature: Everything that appears to us is conditioned by our sensibility and is always already unified and ordered under the categories. Thus, we have no knowledge of things in themselves. All we know are their appearances. Nietzsche follows less Kant than a neo-Kantian position when he maintains that all we are conscious of are mere appearances, appearances that do not guarantee any relation to a thing in itself (Kant never doubted that appearances are appearances of "things themselves"). Like Kant, Nietzsche says that appearances are categorized and schematized, however he will tell a quite different story from Kant's when he replaces Kant's transcendental critique with a genealogical critique and proposes "evolutionary" or "biological" processes that are grounded in struggling forces as leading to these categorizations and schematizations. Thus, bodies and bodily processes appear to become the site through which a world of appearances comes to be.

Especially in the eighties Nietzsche asserts again and again that the categories spring from the necessity to give security and steadfastness to life. Unity, substance, causality, reality, and so on, are fictions that serve the preservation of a specific kind of living being. They originally owe themselves to different constellations of struggling drives and forces that strive for growth and preservation. In section 110 of *The Gay Science* Nietzsche for instance says: "that there are enduring things; that there are equal things; that there are things, substances, bodies; that a thing is what it appears to be; that our will is free; that what is good for me is also good in itself"—these are all "wrong propositions of belief" (*irrtümliche Glaubenssätze*) that proved to be useful and preserving for the humans species.[11] In section 111 he writes:

> Those, for example, who did not know how to find often enough what is "equal" as regards both nourishment and hostile animals—those, in other words, who subsumed things too slowly and cautiously—were favored with a lesser probability of survival than those who guessed immediately upon encountering similar instances that they must be equal.[12]

This way of drawing back principles of understanding to physiological conditions in the widest sense, which Nietzsche performs especially in the eighties, at first presents itself as a mere reversing of Platonism that uses the same structures of thinking that it attempts to overcome. The structures that are maintained are not only the metaphysical opposition between a world of being (ideas, forms, shapes) and a world of becoming (drives, emotions, instincts); they are found as well in the way Nietzsche approaches the world of becoming in his thinking. For instance, when he speaks of physiological conditions that underlie the principles of understanding, he uses exactly these principles of understanding. Nietzsche is well aware of this fact and expresses it in all its radicality. In 1884 he writes the following:

> "Consciousness"—to what extent the represented representation, the represented will, the represented feeling (*the only one we know*) is completely superficial! "Appearance" also our *inner* world![13]

Everything entering our consciousness is already simplified, equalized, schematized, and categorized. This applies also for the so-called inner experience of our body, of our wills and feelings, to which Schopenhauer still granted an immediacy that separated them from the world of representation.

The fact that Nietzsche draws from the very structures of thinking that he attempts to overcome also bears on his explicit understanding of language. He writes:

> The "inner experience" enters our consciousness only after it has found a language which the individual *understands* . . . i.e., a translation of a condition in more *known* ones.[14]

Thus he comprehends language and consciousness in a synonymous way. Everything coming to speech has already undergone a simplifying interpretation. The logical consequence one might draw from this is that also this interpretation by Nietzsche, which conceives consciousness as an organic development, belongs to consciousness, is mere surface, mere representation. The body, too, as we think it and as we consciously feel it is, according to Nietzsche, mere representation, surface without ground. This means that one cannot simply abolish the true world of reason by reversing its relation to the sensible world and by explaining the world of reason to be the product of the sensible world, because the meaning of the sensible world is attached to that of reason. With the true world we abolish also the apparent one.

It appears that Nietzsche points to a way out of this dilemma when he repeatedly claims that thinking cannot be reduced to what enters our consciousness. As Nietzsche says, the greatest part of our mental activities (*geistiges Wirken*) occurs unconsciously, without being felt.[15] Thereby conscious thinking is not separated from the unconscious, but it is, so to speak, its surface. Nietzsche calls consciousness "the last and latest development of the organic."[16] Consciousness is the most superficial and worst part of humans; even more, it is a "disease" because "it does not belong to the individual existence of humans" but "is developed only with respect to the usefulness of the community and the herd."[17] We are conscious only of what is ordinary, what pertains to the "average" in ourselves. We never are conscious of the particular, the unique, the creative aspect of ourselves. We never are conscious of the generating occurrences (*das Wirken*) that are not yet schematized according to general principles.

Still the question remains: How can Nietzsche speak at all of these unconscious occurrences if in the moment he speaks of them he transforms them into mere surface and mere appearance? How can he think them and name them if they are precisely what escapes our consciousness, when even our most intimate feelings cannot grant an immediate access to them? How can we reach at all those unconscious occurrences of which we know only the surface?

b.   The Trace of the Body

For Nietzsche, more than any other phenomenon, what can grant an access to unconscious occurrences is the body. In 1886–87 he writes: "The phenomenon of the body [Leib] is the richer, clearer, more tangible phenomenon: to be preferred methodically without determining anything about its ultimate meaning."[18]

We should keep in mind especially what he says in the end: not to determine anything about the ultimate meaning of the body, because if we did give an ultimate determination to the body, we would again reduce its richness to an interpretation that rests upon a principle of understanding. In some way, then, we should try to leave the meaning of body in suspense as we take the phenomenon of the body—that is, bodily manifestations—as mere indicators.

Similarly to Schopenhauer, Nietzsche conceives the movements in the body to be indicators of the fundamental character of life that essentially escapes representation. In an aphorism of 1885 Nietzsche demands "that wherever we see or guess movement in the body, we should learn to conclude that there is a subjective invisible life belonging to it. Movement is symbolism for the eye; it indicates that something has been felt, willed, thought."[19] How this feeling, willing, and thinking have occurred remains concealed. All that is left to us are bodily traces indicating that something has occurred, an occurrence that withdraws from our consciousness and from our power of cognition.

In contrast to Schopenhauer, for Nietzsche the movement in the body does not lead to a cognizable essential ground of all beings. When Nietzsche speaks of an unconscious struggle of drives[20] and of an instinctive activity[21] from which our thinking springs forth and when he calls these *will to power*, we should not take these as expressions that name an essence—that is, "something" that would be the ground of the world. Each "something" is already a representation. "Will to power" rather names the "how" of occurrences of life, the play of forces that animate life, and that withdraw in the most part from our consciousness.[22]

We get closer to these occurrences of life that can never be grasped as "something" by also applying this difference between the "how" and the "what" to Nietzsche's own thinking and writing. The distinction between the performative character and the propositional character of his thinking is crucial in order to see that Nietzsche does not simply remain caught up in the metaphysics he strives to overcome.[23] At the same time, we should be aware that there is no "how" without a "what." One cannot separate a process of thought from what it thinks. The point is to understand what Nietzsche thinks from within the way in which his thinking occurs.

If we understood Nietzsche's writings simply as propositions concerning certain contents, then he would remain a victim of what he intends to overcome. We would then take the unconscious drives and instincts—the will to power—of which he speaks, as given and represented things, and would constitute again a "true" metaphysical world: the true world of becoming. We get closer to the performative character of Nietzsche's thought above all when we consider his style and when we perform bodily with him the moods and plays of forces that it discloses. If we want to speak of a liberation of the body in Nietzsche's work, then we have to look for it here, in the performative aspect of his thinking and not in objectifying considerations about the body, be it in inner or outer perception.

Nietzsche makes us aware of this performative character by putting into question and ungrounding radically the object of any act of consciousness. Thereby what he ungrounds is not this or that object, but objectivity as a whole;

that is, the objective horizon in which objects find a specific determination and meaning in correlation to a thinking subject. As already mentioned, for Nietzsche every*thing* that enters our consciousness is mere appearance to which nothing real corresponds; it is interpreted according to categories and schemata that do not find any hold in a given fact; it is a mask without a face behind. Nietzsche's style expresses precisely this. Again and again he withdraws any ground from his readers. The means by which he does this are provocation, irony, open contradictions, sudden shifts of mood in different rhythms of phrases which turn upside down what he has just claimed; he does it in expressions like "maybe," "it appears that . . . ," "I may risk the supposition . . ." and in those hypothetical expressions introduced with "what if . . . ?" or "let us suppose . . . ."[24]

One may consider, for instance, section 354 of *The Gay Science* where Nietzsche questions the primacy of consciousness by reducing it to biological conditions of life. The section is introduced with the sentence: "The problem of consciousness (more precisely, of becoming conscious of something) confronts us only when we begin to comprehend how we *could* dispense with it."[25]

All "deductions" that follow this experiment of thinking (*Gedankenexperiment*) are "hypotheses" Nietzsche makes. The reduction of reasoning to biological conditions of life is introduced in this text as a hypothesis that claims no more credibility than the thought that there are things as such, existing independent of our thinking. It is not that relevant for Nietzsche that we believe more one hypothesis than another. But it is crucial that one sees that in his reduction of reasoning to biological conditions he withdraws the basis for his own hypothesis as much as the basis for the hypothesis he is devaluating. He withdraws the basis for his own argument of the primacy of biological conditions of life in a twofold sense: first, because he introduces his argument only as a hypothesis; second, because his argument is the result of an act of consciousness, the very origin of which it is supposed to explain. Further examples of how Nietzsche ungrounds his own thought are the many places where in open contradiction he says that truth is a lie.[26] If truth is a lie, then there are no lies. Thus the proposition "truth is a lie" ungrounds itself.

In his various ways to unground the principles that constitute the objectivity of thinking, Nietzsche, the philosopher of the "dangerous maybes,"[27] puts his readers in a strange suspense. What appears in this suspense is what I call the bodily dimension in Nietzsche's thinking. It names those occurrences that remain covered up when we focus primarily on the object of thinking: sensations, feelings, affects, tensions, and plays of forces. They include aversion, disgust, indignation, and anxiety, together with elevation, liberation, amusement, pleasure, or happiness. Nietzsche would probably supplement this with the remark that all this goes along with a play of muscles and the excitement of nerve centers, and, of course, these "biological" explanations would merely be indicators of physical occurrences that are largely unconscious.

The bodily dimension that is at play in thought is active in all our activities and states of being, appearing more or less clearly. Metaphysics considers it only as a phenomenon that accompanies thinking, a phenomenon, furthermore, that has a rather inhibiting effect on the clarity of thinking. For Nietzsche this bodily dimension is constitutive of thinking and even more: it bears the trace to productive occurrences that essentially withdraw from our representations and that remain abysmal for our ability of representation. What enters our consciousness in the form of perceptions and representations is the surface of this bodily dimension.

We may become aware of the unconscious bodily dimension of thinking through "indirect hearing," to use an expression of Blondel. As he states, Nietzsche does not want the sound that comes first (*Vordergrundklang*), but the resonance, the hidden sound (*Hinterklang*), the color and the tone of the prominent words (*Vordergrundsworte*); that is, the accompanying tones (*Nebentöne*)[28] which, we might add, point to that which remains hidden *in* what is said and thought.

One may reconsider, in the light of these reflections, Nietzsche's predilection of "biological metaphors," to take an expression from Charles Scott.[29] Their function is not only to subvert the logic of metaphysical principles and values, but they also let resound in a peculiar way the bodily dimension that animates both metaphysical principles and Nietzsche's discourse. Biological accounts of life are very distant to the intimacy in which we may experience our own body when we are "immediately" conscious of pain, pleasure, or emotions. Neural activities (understood as such) are strange to the immediacy that characterizes feelings of value that are attached to certain ideas. When Nietzsche traces truth genealogically back to biological conditions of survival he alienates us from the intimacy of embodied values and inflicts upon us a feeling of truth; he disrupts a physical bond, and thus lets emerge this physical bond in the first place. We may lack the philosophical vocabulary that would allow us to give an explanation of how certain ideas take possession of our "guts" but Nietzsche certainly uncovers *that* such physical attachments are formed without us noticing it when he disrupts these attachments or, to be more precise, when he gives expression to such ruptures in the way he describes the formation of values. (We should not forget that Nietzsche turns against values that he himself incorporates and whose shattering he himself experiences. In this respect we will see how Nietzsche's writing cannot be simply understood as the product of a subjective will.)

Since the unconscious part of our thinking can be noticed only through the conscious part, both need to be thought together. Thus the suspension of objectivity does *not* mean its elimination, but only that its "consistency," its value is transformed. Objectivity loses a great deal of its binding force, it fluidifies, so to speak, into a stream of different bodily motions, moods, feelings, and affects; it becomes transparent for the invisible and lets resonate in what is said the unheard.

The invisible and unhearable dimension of thinking is thought as a productive dimension whose effects become visible at the surface. Consciousness delimits just the realm of this surface. Thinking in its productive, originating event is a much larger occurrence. Nietzsche often describes thinking in its hidden productive dimension as a differentiating, organizing, and identifying event—that is, as the constitution of hierarchies of different drives, instincts, affects, and so on. In this process unified structures crystallize in different constellations that then appear at the surface of our consciousness as concepts and images.[30]

In the section "About the Despisers of the Body" in *Zarathustra*, Nietzsche speaks of the body (Leib) as a "great reason" whose "little tool and plaything" is the "small reason"—the "mind." Zarathustra says:

> What the sense senses, what the mind recognizes never has its end in itself. But sense and mind want to persuade you that they are the end of all things; this is how vain they are.[31]

And a little further in the text Zarathustra continues:

> Behind your thoughts and feelings, my brother, stands a mighty ruler, an unknown wise being—his name is self. He indwells your body, he is your body.[32]

The productive, bodily dimension of thinking is never disclosed "as such" or "in the whole," like an essence we might reach. It lies in the performative character of thinking that is essentially particular, finite, and historical. In the next section of this chapter I would like to trace out the particular historical way in which the bodily dimension of Nietzsche's thinking is disclosed in his text.

## c.  The Historicality of Nietzsche's Thought

The suspension of objectivity through the devaluation of metaphysical principles is for Nietzsche a historical event that exceeds his subjective will. Thus, when asking for the bodily dimension of Nietzsche's thinking we need to be aware that he does not understand his thinking as being subjectively "his." In fact, Nietzsche understands the subject as a product of an interpretation that is tied to a specific feeling of reality.

The subject: this is the term for our belief in a unity underlying all the different impulses of the highest feeling of reality.[33]

The subject is not something given, it is something added and invented and projected behind what there is.—Finally, is it then necessary to posit an interpreter behind the interpretation? Even this is invention, hypothesis.[34]

According to Nietzsche, we form an idea of a subject in connection with a highest feeling of reality. He suggests that this feeling is something like a head of a commonality of forces.[35] We tend to identify ourselves with the strongest feeling we have and to ignore all other forces that are at play together with this feeling. Our identification with a highest feeling of reality leads us to believe that there is a substance underlying it, the same substance that is supposedly the author of our thoughts and interpretations.

Nietzsche is well aware that the forces that are at play in our thoughts and feelings are historically formed. In fact Nietzsche thinks in the awareness that "his" thought arises in a historical event that he cannot make or master but that he can and chooses to affirm (*amor fati*). One may say that in this affirmation his thought becomes properly "his" or that his thought takes shape in this affirmation. Nietzsche titles the last chapter of one of his latest writings, *Ecce Homo*, as follows: "Why I Am a Destiny." More astonishing than the boldness of this title is probably that Nietzsche is right if we consider the enormous and still lasting effects of his work, effects it could not have had if it did not address our histories. Nietzsche starts this chapter with the following words:

I know my fate. One day the memory of something monstrous will be attached to my name—the memory of a crisis like there has been none on this earth before, a deep collision of conscience, the memory of a decision that was evoked *against* everything that had been believed, demanded, and kept holy.[36]

The crisis that Nietzsche proclaims here concerns the loss of fundamental principles that structure Christian-metaphysical lives, including his own. Even if Nietzsche's words may sound to our contemporary ears heavily exaggerated, they do express a historical event, a historical crisis that shatters and transforms bodies in that it shatters and transforms values that have shaped bodies over centuries. The devaluation of metaphysical values is not something Nietzsche decides to do (for whatever reason) but it is first of all something that occurs to him and that as it occurs to him he chooses to affirm.

By putting into question metaphysical principles like God, truth, identity, good and bad, Nietzsche turns against values that he himself embodies. He does not do this because of strongly developed masochistic tendencies but because he experiences how these principles, that appear to be necessities for life, now turn against life and its creative powers. (He laid this out especially in his *Genealogy of Morals*.) It now appears that the only way to free these creative powers again is to devaluate and overcome the embodied metaphysical principles.[37] For Nietzsche the creative powers of life are a form of art, which implies that art is not a primarily human fabrication or endeavor but that it essentially belongs to life. He conceives art as belonging to life already in his early writing "The Birth of Tragedy" where he discusses it in terms of the relation between the Apollynian and the Dionysian, that is, between an artistic energy that produces images (Apollynian) and a transgressive force of excess and dissolution (Dionysian). We find the intertwined forces of the Apollynian and the Dionysian again in the shattering and overcoming of old values and in the creation of new ones.[38]

For Nietzsche, life includes at once the necessity to preserve and the necessity to overcome and create. With respect to creation he also speaks of growth. Furthermore, he stresses that growth has priority with respect to preservation:

A living thing seeks above all to *discharge* its strength—life itself is *will to power*; self-preservation is only one of the indirect and most frequent results.[39]

But in order to release their power living things need resistance:

The will to power can express itself only through *resistances*.[40]

Nietzsche argues in a similar way in an aphorism of 1888:

What every human being wants, what every smallest part of a living organism wants is an increase of power. Striving for this brings along as its consequence pleasure or displeasure; because of this will it [each smallest part of a living organism] looks for a resistance, it needs something which opposes itself.[41]

Nietzsche finds this resistance in the breaking down of metaphysical values. And the counterforces to metaphysical values grow precisely in the overcoming (not in having already overcome) of the resistances posed by these embodied values.

Will to power manifests itself in an internal struggle. This is why Nietzsche speaks always of an inner countermovement when he speaks of will to power. He speaks of resistance and elevation, of preservation and growth, of making constant and overcoming. In response to Heidegger's interpretation of Nietzsche, scholars have again and again pointed out that will to power is not a metaphysical concept that designates the essence of life. Will to power is not simply another name for Schopenhauer's metaphysical will but rather designates ways in which life occurs. Thus, it is always particularized and includes an impenetrable complexity that exceeds intellectual grasp.

This complexity is not the only reason why the will to power cannot be conceived as a metaphysical principle. Another reason is that for Nietzsche the character of the world as a whole is chaos.[42] Chaos is not simply opposed to will to power but rather is constitutive for the creative aspect of will to power.

The will to power occurs in an overcoming of something consistent. This overcoming leads to the downfall or destruction (*Untergang*) of what was consistent. This implies a moment of a lack of order and ground, a moment of chaos. This is precisely the moment of the devaluation of objectivity, when the whole relation to the world is shaken and begins to dissolve. Thus, the creative character of life is intimately connected with its abysmal character or with what Nietzsche calls chaos. It implies a continuous re-creation in the decline of what is in its consistency. This re-creation does not occur according to a general model but rather in different rhythms, in different speeds, in unpredictable breaks and fragments, and sometimes also in the reconstitution of similar orders.

But there is a major manifestation of will to power which—in Nietzsche's experience—opposes itself to its own downfall and thus to its creative movement, namely metaphysics. By posing highest unchangeable principles metaphysics negates the perishing belonging to life and therefore negates life itself.

"One must still have chaos in oneself to be able to give birth to a dancing star," says Nietzsche's Zarathustra in his opening speech. But "alas," he continues, "the time will come when man will no longer give birth to a star."[43] This is the time of the last human being who has no more chaos in himself and is not ready for his downfall, the time of that human being that dully glides on the surface of life, comforting herself in the certainty of those principles that once were generated as a necessity of life. One can imagine as a prototype of this kind of being humans in Aldous Huxley's *Brave New World*: Humans in a technically (almost) completely secured and organized world who suffocate possible uneasy thoughts in the very moment they germinate. The appearance of the last human being represents the utmost possibility of life turning against itself, against its creative character.

Nietzsche says that in order to grow, to create, one needs to have chaos in oneself. Thereby the relation between overcoming and chaos, both of which belong to life, may be sought in that turning point where what was established is devaluated or loses its power. It may be sought in that moment when the fundament one was used to rely on withdraws, when what is to come is still in it's becoming. I interpret this moment as the moment of suspension of objectivity by a radical questioning of fundamental values and principles that constitute the objective horizon of our relation to objects. In this moment appears the bodily dimension of our lives.

The fact that Nietzsche experiences the fundamental character of life to be will to power implies that he also experiences his own thinking as will to power, as a setting of new values in the overcoming of old ones. The resistances against which he strives in an attempt to overcome embodied values are probably, as always, manifold and complex. Yet there are two focal points of resistance one may point out: First the suffering that according to Nietzsche underlies all metaphysics—the suffering because of the finitude of life, because everything in life passes away. In order to escape this suffering humans flee into the hope of a better life to come, a life of truth, consistency, justice, and happiness. The second focal point is probably stronger than the first; it is the suffering of metaphysical suffering itself, the overcoming of which Nietzsche thinks as he affirms the eternal recurrence of the same. For Nietzsche, the metaphysical denial of life becomes a resistance that he attempts to overcome by affirming what metaphysics turned against: the finite character of life. The most radical way of affirming this finitude and becoming is to will it again and again in its eternal recurrence.[44]

## d.   Transformations of Bodies

In the affirmation of the eternal recurrence, the relation to the world, the bodily way of being in the world, changes. In this moment thinking twists free from Platonism, conceived as the consequence of the reactive character of metaphysics, that is, of the reaction to the finitude of life. Platonism is characterized by a fundamental tension between becoming (passing away) and being in the sense of permanent presence, so that being acquires its consistency in opposition and resistance to becoming. The fundamental tension between being and becoming is, so to speak, the yoke that harnesses any metaphysical understanding of the world, the yoke that harnesses the bodily dimension of metaphysical thinking and in this way finds a hold in life. This fundamental tension is introduced in Platonist thinking by the ethical demand to turn toward the unchangeable forms in resistance to the bodily motions of the psyche[45] and takes different shapes in the history of metaphysics. In the last phase of metaphysics, the stage of the last human, the fundamental tension between being and becoming stiffens up to the point where the relation to becoming is no longer perceived. As Nietzsche says, the last human has no more chaos in him/herself;

he/she has no chaos to escape by setting a metaphysical world, and even less a chaos that he/she affirms.

The overcoming of the reactive character of life in the affirmation of the eternal recurrence of the same has been interpreted by Heidegger as a completion of subjectivity and as the beginning of an era of mere arbitrariness. The loss of the fundamental metaphysical tension seems to result for him in a loss of the roots (the truth) of being. Luce Irigaray also suggests that the eternal recurrence is a movement that in closing in on itself excludes the other[46] and spins eternally in a void. By exposing what his discourse excludes she also reminds us that, even if we consider Nietzsche's thought as not being subjectively his, Nietzsche's story is not everybody's story, his passion not everybody's passion. Part of Heidegger's and Irigaray's approach to Nietzsche is that they do not imply an ultimate judgment regarding Nietzsche but arise out of quite singular intimate engagements with his thought that keep his thought in question.[47]

Along this space of questioning I will briefly consider possibilities that may arise in the moment of the twisting free from metaphysics in the affirmation of life in its becoming and thus also passing away. In a Nietzschean understanding, the positive effect of the overcoming of the two-world order is that chaos and becoming demand and free new possibilities of life. A thought and way of being that has twisted free from metaphysics would be neither structured by a need to overcome the finitude of life nor by the need to overcome a resistance to this finitude. A suffering of the finitude of life and moments and forms of resistances to it may still be at play, but they would not dominate the way our bodies and the bodily dimension in thought are structured. One could imagine how a creative play of different formations and constellations of forces becomes possible that does not rely on a last principle and does not lead to an ultimate end. What would prevent this play from being simply arbitrary is that it remains bound to specific embodied values, behaviors, and beliefs. These embodied values would not have the power of highest principles or criteria of truth but would be experienced in their becoming. With respect to the bodily dimension of thinking, this would entail an intensified awareness for bodily tensions, emotions, movements, drives, and power plays. And is it not the case that when we pay attention to forces and motions at play in our lives, there are moments that cannot be reduced to the economy of domination and obedience or to resentment against the finitude of life? What about relaxation, unexpected moments of love, or simply indifference? What about ways of being with others, with plants, animals, and ourselves that are not about desire or power, that in fact are *about* nothing, but that express forms of sharing rhythms and spaces? Maybe the two-world theory has always been a fable, a fable that certainly is suggestive and has had its effects on concrete lives.

e.    Conclusion

If we take a look at Nietzsche's thinking of the will to power in the light of the overcoming of the fundamental tension of metaphysics, it appears that he remains to a great extent at the threshold of an overcoming of metaphysics. The thought of the eternal recurrence of the same is a thought Nietzsche announces in *Zarathustra* as the most difficult thought. It is not clear whether Nietzsche was ever able to think it in such a way that he underwent the transformation this thought announces. Nietzsche performs a devaluation of metaphysical values in the various ways in which he suspends the metaphysical relations to objects through irony, reversal, shifts in mood, and contradictions. But what he says is largely a critique of metaphysics and thus remains under its power. This is part of the historicality in which his thinking arises. However, we do owe to Nietzsche an opening of the performative aspect of thought and with it of the bodily dimension in thought, an opening that has profoundly affected and continues to affect contemporary thought. We saw how in Nietzsche's texts this opening occurs in the overturning and ungrounding of embodied metaphysical values and thus in an exposure to chaos that gives space to the creation of new values or simply new forms of life. This moment of chaos resonates with *Timaeus'* chora,[48] as both have the character of an originary opening. However, the bodily dimension in thinking that emerges through this opening is different in the two philosophers. Plato's text moves toward a differencing of body and thinking as the movements of the psyche gather toward the same. In Nietzsche's text, the recurrence of chaos disperses preformed conceptualities and values into a multiplicity of forces.

# PART TWO

# At the Limits of Phenomenology

## Two Phenomenological
## Accounts of the Body

Despite the fact that it remains related to Cartesianism, the phenomenological movement, as founded by Husserl and developed afterward by German and French philosophers, makes a decisive step in reopening thinking to the world in its phenomenal richness and with this to bodies and ways of thinking bodily. This movement leaves behind the neo-Kantian epistemological trap framed by the distinction between the thing as it appears and the thing in itself. Phenomenology turns to the world of appearances, describing appearances both in the direction of the manifold ways in which they appear objectively (as things immediately present, or imagined, or remembered, etc.) and in the direction of how they are given or constituted in acts of consciousness or perception (acts of thinking, willing, feeling). By conceiving what is thought or perceived always in correlative unity with the act of thinking or perceiving (the *intentio-intentum* correlation) phenomenology, in principle, overcomes the split between the world of consciousness and the world of things "outside" consciousness that Descartes articulates as the division between a thinking substance (*res cogitans*) and an extended substance (*res extensa*). Bodies become phenomena of philosophical inquiry not only as body-objects (Körper), but also as lived bodies (Leib) in correlation to acts of thought and perception that include bodily (kinaesthetic) movements.

One could argue that by overcoming the split between appearance and thing in itself, Nietzsche's problematic of the overcoming of a two-world order becomes obsolete. Who cares whether behind the appearing object lies a true object or not! Is phenomenology not perfectly happy with the surface, with how things appear *for* a subject?

However, from a Nietzschean perspective, one can easily reply that in phenomenology still persists the shadow of the old god of metaphysics. Does phenomenology, especially Husserl's transcendental phenomenology (after the transcendental turn in *Ideas I*), not still believe in a subject-unity? Does phenomenology not perpetuate the belief in truth when it speaks of the immediate presence of an object in its self-givenness? One could argue that Husserlian phenomenology is an extreme form of Cartesianism, a witness to the triumph of subjectivity that we find celebrated when Hegel's spirit realizes itself after having sublimated (*aufgehoben*) all negativity. Now, there is no more "outside" to consciousness, our whole concern now is how things appear within consciousness. Whereas in Descartes and Kant there at least was a sense of something escaping consciousness (god, things in themselves, i.e., bodies), now all that counts is what presents itself to consciousness and—in the case of Husserl's transcendental philosophy—this is even conceived as being constituted in consciousness.

One should note however, that the later Husserl develops the notion of an "operative intentionality," that is, of an opening of consciousness to the outside that allows for consciousness to constitute phenomena objectively. Even Husserl's phenomenology does not exhaust itself in the clarity of a theoretical self-consciousness. In its later stage it starts merging into the opaqueness of the life-world from which all philosophical reflection emerges. When phenomenology turns to the question of its own genesis in the life-world, it rediscovers the lived body and with it an otherness at its very heart. Subjectivity dissolves from within and thinking finds itself emerging in a living engagement with the world. Thus, phenomenology, like Nietzsche's philosophy, is a threshold at which reemerges the bodily dimension in thinking, and, with it, an opening to, or rather within the world. Although it remains tied to a subject-object structure that limits the accounts of the bodily dimension in thinking, phenomenology is a threshold that allows different ways of thinking to emerge (for instance Heidegger's thought or contemporary French thought).

The following chapters discuss the most thought-provoking texts with respect to the issues of the bodily dimension in thinking. It considers two quite different phenomenological thinkers, Max Scheler and Maurice Merleau-Ponty. Max Scheler originally was not a Husserl scholar (he studied with neo-Kantian Rickert) but became part of the phenomenology circle of Munich. He therefore combines more traditional neo-Kantian elements with phenomenological analyses. In many ways his thought of a "*Wesensschau*" recalls Plato's eidetic seeing. However, in distinction to Plato, Scheler makes also very acute and careful analyses of the body that take him to the limits of his own thought. As is the case with Plato's *Timaeus*, Scheler's late text *Man's Place in Nature* allows for a reading that accounts for the emerging of a distinction between the body, or a bodily dimension, and thinking or spirit (Geist) in thought. But Scheler's text also allows for a further articulation of the bodily dimension in thinking than is to be found in the *Timaeus*. Some Nietzschean themes recur both in his thought that the body is an analyser for perception and in his thought that the life of thinking is rooted in most basic impulses that we share with the most primitive life forms on earth.

Merleau-Ponty's *The Visible and the Invisible* (chapter 4) certainly is the most far-reaching work in terms of a phenomenology of the body. In fact the issue of the human lived body (Leib) is embedded in the larger and more fundamental issues of the flesh of the world. This suggests that in Merleau-Ponty the bodily dimension in thinking is finally no longer centered in subjectivity and consciousness. Rather, the "reflection" that inquires into the bodily dimension in thinking is understood to arise not in the human mind but in what Merleau-Ponty calls the chiasm that articulates the flesh of the world and the flesh of the lived body.

One may say that in a certain way Merleau-Ponty and Scheler are at opposite ends of the phenomenological movement; Scheler is still influenced by a classical ontology that draws a sharp distinction between essence and existence, whereas Merleau-Ponty breaches the limits of phenomenology with an ontology that does not operate with this distinction. The latter has, however, its own limitations that are tied to the primacy of perception and with it to a form of reflexive thought that merges into the distinction of subject and object, a distinction that at the same time Merleau-Ponty begins to overcome.

*Chapter Three*

# Driven Spirit
## The Body in Max Scheler's Phenomenology

Scheler's phenomenology and, more specifically, his phenomenological analyses of the body are not getting much attention in contemporary continental philosophy. The reason might be that in contemporary thinking, the question of the body arises together with an attempt at overcoming a metaphysical dualism of body and mind. It may seem that Scheler holds on to such a dualism, because his idea of spirit (Geist) simply appears to repeat a traditional notion of a disembodied metaphysical principle. Even if one may argue that the notion of a mutual penetration of life and spirit in Scheler's later works resists such a reduction, Scheler never undertook the "Nietzschean" step of understanding spirit as a form of life. Instead he maintained that—even in its relatedness and dependency on life—spirit originates precisely in distinction to life. For Scheler, spirit has a distinct principle.

Wherever one may stand regarding the question of whether or not Scheler is a metaphysical dualist (and in what sense), his rich analysis of the body certainly challenges a simple dualism and opens ways of understanding "body" in quite differentiated and original ways. Similarly to Plato, in fact, Scheler's differentiations between life and spirit makes visible aspects of the bodily dimension in thinking that otherwise may remain obscured.

In this chapter I consider Scheler's phenomenology of the body in its relation to thinking (spirit). I will show how he succeeds in avoiding a simple objectification of the body, which would reduce it, on Nietzschean terms, to an object of consciousness that necessarily fails to describe or think the phenomenon of the body as such (prior to its being simply an object of consciousness). As we will see, instead of conceiving the body as an object of consciousness, Scheler thinks of it as an analyzer that determines if and how something comes to consciousness. I will also show how Scheler's late thought of the "powerlessness of the spirit" (*die Machtlosigkeit des Geistes*) as it is presented in *Man's Place in Nature* (*Die Stellung des Menschen im Kosmos*) not only leads to an overcoming of the dualism between mind and body but puts into question the separate principles Scheler claims for life and spirit. This latter point requires that one not only considers what Scheler apparently intends to say, but also the *enactment* of his thinking. Thus, in my encounter with Scheler's thought, by remaining sensible to the way his thinking moves, I move beyond what Scheler explicitly says.

Thus, the aim of this chapter is neither simply to give an accurate interpretation of Scheler's philosophical understanding of "body," nor to argue that Scheler did not go far enough in his thinking or missed acknowledging necessary consequences of his thinking. Rather, again, it is to open, with Scheler's text, possibilities to think the bodily dimension in thinking. As in the previous chapter, I will consider not only what the philosopher says but also how his thinking moves in the text, thus questioning the unsaid in the saying, the unthought in thinking. However, even in going beyond what the philosopher explicitly affirms, a productive encounter with the philosopher still requires that one engage his writings and understand his intentions. We shall therefore first consider some basic features of Scheler's phenomenology.

a.   The Phenomenological Attitude

Scheler understands phenomenology[1] not as a method in the sense of an "intellectual procedure concerning facts"[2] *(Denkverfahren über Tatsachen),* but as an "attitude of spiritual seeing"[3] (*Einstellung des geistigen Schauens*). This attitude differs considerably from what we usually call observation. In observing something, what is observed is conceived as being independent of the observer. Not so in the phenomenological attitude, where a phenomenon is lived or experienced (*er-lebt*)[4] and spiritually seen (*er-schaut*) "only in the *living* and *seeing act itself*, in its enactment."[5] What is experienced and seen (*das Er-lebte und Er-schaute*) "appears *in* and only in it [the act]."[6] Insofar as it is experienced, the spiritually seen phenomenon is not simply an objective matter of fact, but it is woven into the occurrence of our life. It involves (we will have to see how) our physicality, our feelings, sensations, drives, and instincts.

Scheler insists: "The first thing which [ ... ] a philosophy founded on phenomenology must possess as its basic character is the most lively, most intense and *most immediate experiential commerce with the world itself*—i.e., with the things which are in concern."[7]

Thereby the reflective gaze of the phenomenologist dwells "solely in the place where lived experience and object world touch each other."[8] This place is what we may call in Husserlian terms the jointure of *intentio* and *intentum*, of act and object in their inseparable correlative unity. We may keep this in mind when reading Scheler's text.

The phenomenological attitude differs from our daily "natural" attitude as well as from a scientific attitude. It requires a specific reduction that in Scheler differs somewhat with respect to the Husserlian reduction.[9] In his phenomenological investigations Scheler "puts into brackets" and thus suspends two things: First, "the *real enactment* [*realer Aktvollzug*] of an act and all its accompanying phenomena, which do not lie in the sense and in the direction of the act itself; as well as all properties of its carrier (animal, human, God)."[10] This means that he suspends also our psychophysical properties and the role they might play in an act. Second, he suspends "all *positing* (belief or disbelief) *of the specificity of the coefficient of reality*"[11] that is, whether something is mere appearance or reality. Therefore the phenomenological investigation is directed only to the *essence*, that is, the "whatness" in distinction to the existence (*Dasein*) of something. Such essences (*Wesenheiten*) are, for instance, the essences "glass," "human being," "tree," and also "body," independently of whether they are only represented or directly perceived through our eyes.

One can find the sharp distinction between essence and existence throughout Scheler's writings. One might ask how Scheler can sustain this distinction in the face of what he said earlier with respect to the phenomenological attitude. How can I not consider the real enactment of an act and thus the existence of something, if in the phenomenological attitude we should thematize that which is seen *in* the experiencing (living) act? In suspending the existence as well as the psychophysical constitution of the carrier of an act (of my own psychophysical constitution) do I not lose exactly the lived experience (*das Erleben*) *in* which what is phenomenologically questioned is given to me? And if, according to Scheler, this is not the case, then how are we to understand the "lived experience"?

Even though the German word "Erleben" is made up in part by the word "leben," which means life, Scheler has an understanding of the word in question that is precisely distinguished from life. The experience in which something is given to a spiritual seeing, is spiritual as well.[12] According to Scheler, the spirit (Geist) designates everything that has the nature (*Wesen*) of act, intentionality, and fulfillment of sense (*Sinnerfülltheit*)[13] It includes reason, thinking of ideas (*Ideendenken*), intuition of primordial phenomena, and essential contents and "a specific class of volitional and emotional acts such as generosity (*Güte*), love, awe, spiritual wondering, happiness, despair."[14] All these, as well as willing, remembering, and imagining, are modes of "Erleben" of any concrete act. In Scheler's understanding, these feelings, acts of will, and so on, are in their very nature (Wesen) distinct from life in its psychophysical constitution. This implies that they are distinct from our body considered as a physical organism and its physical drives such as desire for food, sex, power, and so on.

Phenomenological investigation suspends the psychophysical constitution of the carrier of an act as well as the real enactment of an act and all its accompanying phenomena that do not lie in the sense and in the direction of the act itself. What lies in the sense and in the direction of the act itself is determined by what directs an act. Absolute measure of any act of knowledge, and thus also of the intentional direction of the act is, according to Scheler, "the *self-givenness* of a fact (*Selbstgegebenheit eines Tatbestandes . . .*) in evident conformity of the intended and of what is given in the experience (seeing) exactly as it is intended [*in der evidenten Deckungseinheit des Gemeinten und des genau so wie gemeint auch im Erleben gegebenen*]."[15] At the same time, the phenomenological fact is given purely in itself only when "nothing of the form, function, selective moment, method, not to speak of an organization of the carrier of an act, lies in-between the pure idea of an act and the object [*Gegenstand*]."[16] Scheler calls such a purely self-given fact "absolute existence" (*absolutes Dasein*). Thus, that which determines a phenomenological act lies beyond any psychophysical determination; what determines a phenomenological act is pure existence.

The problem here is that this absolute measure is as unachievable as the absolute self-givenness of a phenomenological fact. While maintaining the sharp distinction between spirit and life, and while asserting that phenomenological investigation should suspend all relation to our psychophysical constitution, Scheler thinks that no human intuition and cognition can be purely spiritual and no object of human intuition and cognition can be given purely in itself. He says that all human intuition and cognition remains *relative to life* (*Daseinsrelativ*); that is, it remains bound to the carrier of an act and his psychophysical organization. Scheler proves here to be a true platonic thinker, and by this I mean a thinker who like Plato experiences thinking as always occurring in the middle of life with all its contingencies and drives, while suggesting that the origin of ideas is reached in resistance to life.[17] But in distinction to Plato, Scheler makes a considerable phenomenological analysis of the role our psychophysical constitution plays in human perception and understanding. Of course, in doing so, he elevates this constitution to a phenomenological fact, to an object of phenomenological inquiry.[18]

In his phenomenology, Scheler makes a clear distinction between spirit and body, between essences and existence. But we have also seen that these distinctions are relativized when Scheler speaks of the importance of lived experience for phenomenology and of the fact that all cognition remains relative to life.

## b. The Lived Body as Analyzer of Inner and Outer Perception

As Husserl, Scheler distinguishes between Leib, the "lived body," and Körper, the body conceived as an extended object among others (often translated as object-body). But he also makes further differentiations. According to Scheler, at first the lived body (Leib) is a psychophysically indifferent fact (*Gegebenheit*) appearing differently in internal and external perception. In external perception it appears to us as "body-object" (*Leibkörper*). If I look at my hand it looks like an object similar to other objects in the world. In internal perception my body is given to me as "body-soul" (*Leibseele*). This includes sensations like hunger, pleasure, pain, kinesthetical sensations of place and movement, and sensations of resistance in muscles, tendons, and joints.[19]

Even though Scheler classifies the lived body as belonging to the sphere of objects[20] (to the world) and thus as having a correlative relation to the spirit, the determination he gives to the lived body does not treat it as an object. In *The Nature of Sympathy* he conceives the lived body as an analyzer that determines what of the whole content of psychical and physical phenomena is brought up—that is, which psychic and physical phenomena are brought to our consciousness. This way of conceiving the body allows Scheler to maintain the distinction between essence and existence: The body does not determine the content of "being this or that way" (*Soseinsgehalt*) of a perception, but only its separation, selection, and "manifestation" (*Abhebung*).[21]

Every perception is accompanied by motion impulses (*Bewegungsimpulse*) and sensations (*Empfindungen*). But neither these nor changes in the nerve system, which might be objectively shown, cause the content of a perception. They only condition *if and how* this content is given. In external perception, for instance, our senses give us only perspectives on a perceived object. Strictly speaking, when I look at the tree outside my window, I see only a part of it. I do not see the back of the tree and I see the tree as it appears to me only when I raise my head and look at it. Yet in my perception the tree is given to me as a whole. Therefore my senses condition the way in which I perceive the tree but they are not the cause of the tree nor do they explain how I can perceive the tree *as such*.

Something similar is true of interior perception that is always mediated by what Scheler calls "inner sense" (*innerer Sinn*). The inner sense refers to variations of the body through which psychical phenomena become contents of perception. The variations of the body have corresponding variations in the nerve processes in the "body-object" and in modifications of the "body-soul," and they select what from the total psychic experience appears in inner consciousness.[22] In other words, the variations of the one phenomenon called "lived body" appear differently in interior or exterior perception.

For example, a psychical content like the joy caused by the visit of a friend is mediated by variations of my body that I might sense in interior perception by feeling energized and excited, and that can be localized in exterior perception through objectively measurable nerve processes. Another example could refer to memories that come back through a particular bodily sensation, which I associate with a certain past event. Thinking in general is mediated by body variations.

The inner sense "dissociates" thoughts, feelings, and expectations into specific contents that follow in a certain order. In Scheler's understanding phenomena belonging to the soul (phenomena of internal perception) are in one another (*ineinander*) and become distinct contents only through the inner sense that dissociates them.[23]

Scheler distinguishes the aspects mediated by the body not only from an essential content but also from the experience in which any perception and cognition takes place. He distinguishes the body from experience: "The body in its 'variations' is only condition for the looks, the 'aspects' that our experience (*Erleben*) takes for the inner sense, but never for this experience itself."[24]

Thus, according to Scheler the lived body does not contribute in any way to the content of an intentional act; neither to the essence perceived nor to the experience in which it is perceived. Even more: the lived body has the tendency to cover up the content of an intentional act because it has the tendency to give primacy to what is important for its drive structure (*Triebstruktur*).[25] The more one follows this tendency and thus "lives in the body," [26] the more one lives according to bodily appetites and the less one is able to see essences themselves and to let oneself be guided by spiritual feelings like love, generosity, and awe.

Even though Scheler maintains a sharp distinction between body and spirit, and between the mediations of essences (the ways they are given) and essences themselves, there are points of interference between the two. On the one hand the body is necessary in order for essences to be seen and experienced, on the other hand the lived body has a tendency to overtake the scene by putting forward that which helps to satisfy its desires and needs. How is it possible, then, to distinguish spirit (act) and body that clearly? Does Scheler simply posit this distinction as an unachievable ideal? But if we want to follow Scheler's claim that phenomenology questions the place where lived experience and object world touch each other and that a phenomenon can be seen and experienced only in the living experience of an act, then we should ask: *How can we understand from within the experience of a phenomenological act the difference between body and spirit?*

With this question the present interpretation of Scheler shifts from following what he says to considering how what he said is enacted in his thinking. I am now moving (beyond what Scheler explicitly says) toward exploring how we might understand *from within* the experience of an act (i.e., in the enactment of thinking) the differentiation Scheler makes between spirit and body. For this purpose I will consider how Scheler describes a particular experience of the "I" (a psychic phenomenon) in distinction to body modifications in *Formalism in Ethics and Non-Formal Ethics of Values*:

> There is a state which language calls "*gathering*," i.e., a concentrated 'being-in-oneself'—so to speak a "living deep inside oneself." In this state it seems that our total spiritual life [*seelisches Leben*], and this in-cludes also the spiritual life of our past, is gathered in *one* and acts as *one*; these are rare moments—for example before major decisions and actions. In these moments one does not remember anything "particular" from previous experiences—but somehow everything is "there" and "effective" [*wirksam*]. At the same time, we are not empty, but completely "full" and "rich." Here, we are really with "ourselves." [. . .] We overlook our *whole* I in all its variety or we experience how it gathers as a whole in *one* act, one action, one deed, one work. [. . .] For all those who know the phenome-non, this is connected with a very characteristic way in which *the body is given*. The own corporeality is given as something "belonging" to that concentrated totality and over which the concentrated totality can exer-cise "*power*" and dominance. At the same time, the corporeality is given as "only present" and as being a moment that is included in an existence that is given as "permanent." In this experience the momentary content of the corporeality somehow seems to flow by this permanent existence.[27]

After this passage, Scheler contrasts this particular experience to what he calls a "living in the body." To be gathered in the I as described above indicates a state in which a phenomenon is given with no interference of body modifications that would dissociate the totality of the experience. The endurance of the gath-ering that allows me to perceive the totality of the I is described by Scheler as being in contrast with the flowing-by of the body modifications. In this sense, we might say that the I is experienced as being independent from the body. The two seem to be two discernible essences. But we might also consider that being totally gathered in oneself has a specific relation to body modifications. This leads to the consideration that that which allows me to perceive the permanence of the spir-itual gathering is precisely the flow of body modifications. The very fact that Scheler speaks of the endurance (or permanence) of the experienced phenome-non *in* the experience (and not of a timelessness of the experienced phenomenon or of its eternity) implies a temporal sense of the gathering in the I that is given in the flowing-by of body modifications. This specific temporality of the gathering in the I seems to occur as a temporal differencing from the flowing-by of body modifications. The gathering in the I does not ultimately separate itself from body modifications but is experienced in relation to them. Further, the temporal differencing in the gathering into the I occurs with a sense of dominance, of elevation over (and within) our bodily state. This motion of elevation may be considered as a spacing (an opening of space) that occurs together with the differencing. Thus the gathering into the I occurs in the opening of a spatiotemporal dimension of being.

If we would want to give a name to this spatiotemporal differencing, which would describe its character with reference to the spiritual gathering in the I on the one hand and to the flowing-by of the body-modifications on the other, we could neither exclude its bodily or its spiritual character, nor could we attribute it simply to one of the two or to both together. Scheler does not explicitly think this spatiotemporal differencing. He focuses on what comes out of it.

This differencing cannot properly be thought as an essence, a "whatness," because it is prior to it. It can only be experienced in an act. In Scheler's thought, what cannot be thought as a "whatness" and at the same time is act in which essences can be "seen" is spirit. If the differencing that we find in the experience of the gathering in ourselves is what Scheler calls "Geist," spirit, then we have to say that this spirit is experienced bodily; it is experienced in the flowing-by of bodily motions. We should note, however, that in saying this we not only think spirit differently from Scheler, but also the term "bodily." The latter term indicates the sensible quality of the spatiotemporal dimension that we experience in the act of thinking.

Another example Scheler gives to illustrate the difference between body and spirit might be more interesting for our concerns. He gives an example concerning the "timely boundaries of my body."[28] Scheler says that "it belongs to the body as it is given that it fills up [*erfüllt*] its presence, its 'now-here'."[29] This "now-here" is a condition for objective time (the time we measure) insofar as the moments following one upon another in measurable time are conceived analogously to the present points of our life as they are experienced in the presence of our body. But the spirit, Scheler says, "swings over the limit of presence [and thus of the body] in two directions: In the attitude of *remembrance* I go into the past and little by little the past world appears before my spiritual eye; and similarly in *expecting* I spiritually dwell in the contents of my future."[30]

Scheler would certainly concede that our memories and expectations are related to our body. But, according to him, what the body does in these instances is just to cause the selection of our memories or expectations. *What* I remember or expect as well as the *act* of remembering or expecting remains, in his view, utterly different from bodily motions. Consider, for instance, an example of a woman who through a specific Asian technique of massage was brought back to the memory of being abused as a child. This memory seemed to have appeared just by releasing certain muscular tensions in her body. However Scheler would say that it is not the body that has the memory of child abuse, but that the body only determines that this memory is brought back. What is brought back in memory and the act in which it is brought back remain separate from the body motions that released the memory.

Now, again one may ask what happens to this differentiation between spirit and body when we pay attention to the performativity of thought and ask: How does Scheler *experience* the difference between body motions and spirit? *How does he perceive and think the excess of the spiritual act* over body modifications?

In order to perceive this excess, his thinking as well as ours has to *reflect* upon the act of remembering and expecting. In doing this, the lived body becomes the object of the reflective act. It appears as something being present now and distinct from *what* is remembered and expected as well as from the spiritual acts of remembering and expecting. In reflecting upon an act of memory, the act itself withdraws from objectification. As Scheler puts it, reflective knowledge only "accompanies" the act. We may also speak of an awareness of the act that does not conceptualize it or place it in any way before our intellectual sight. (Remember that for Scheler, any act is in itself spiritual; and spirit is anything having the nature of act, intentionality, and sense—meaning.) Thus, in a phenomenological reflection on an act of memory a differencing occurs, a shaping and appearing of different elements of perception. There appears *the intended object* of an act (for example "what" we have a memory of), there appears the *body* as what separates and brings forth a specific content of perception (for example, that specific memory that is linked to a certain sensation I have right now), and there is the movement of reflection, the *intending act*, that withdraws from objectification.

But on what grounds can Scheler maintain that the act itself is spiritual in the sense that it excludes the lived body? Did not Scheler say in *Formalism in Ethics* that the gathering in the I (a spiritual act) occurs in distinction to the passing flow of bodily motions? And does this constant flow of bodily motions not withdraw from objectification? Does it not resist, by its very nature, the sense of a presence that can be somehow grasped? To properly objectify our bodily motions we need to look at them as if from exterior perception. But then we already have lost this constant flow of bodily motions as we sense it in interior perception.

In phenomenological reflection we also sense a physical withdrawal, we sense bodily motions that we are not able to properly objectify. Further, the body in its quality of being an analyzer seems to escape objectification as well. The separating and selecting performed by the body, as we experience it in a phenomenological act, is not something we could bring before our mind as an object of understanding. We only objectify the result of this selective operation. The movement of nerves and muscles that we can measure with appropriate equipment only covers one aspect of the function of the body and is not attained in the experience of perceiving and thinking itself.

This leads me to ask the following questions: Does "spirit" designate the *generating movement* of a perception or intuition *or* is Scheler's understanding of spirit the *result* of a reflective act that in this reflection separates the movement of the act from bodily motions by objectifying them? In other words, is the distinction of spirit and body a result—and thus not a principle—of a specific phenomenological reflection?

In order to answer these questions I will turn to Scheler's late work *Man's Place in Nature*. A major topic of this book is the difference as well as connection between spirit and life. In the following, I will—again—not only point out "what" Scheler thinks when he differentiates life and spirit, but also how this difference develops in his writing. This later consideration will lead to a questioning of this differentiation.

## c.   Spirit and Life

Scheler begins his book *Man's Place in Nature* with an exposition of different levels of psychical forces that constitute the biopsychical world. Although these levels for the most part follow the traditional pattern of differentiating plants, animals, and humans in an hierarchical order, Scheler distinguishes more levels of the biopsychical world. Similar to Leibniz, higher forms of life integrate all the characteristics of the lower forms. Scheler's aim is to show that in human life we can find a psychical force that differs *essentially* from all the other psychical forces. Thus, he distinguishes two main classes: the "vital sphere" (*Vitalsphäre*) and the spirit sphere, or we might just say: "life" and "spirit."

The different levels of biopsychic force that Scheler distinguishes are (1) emotional impulse (*Gefühlsdrang*); (2) instinct in the sense of a behavior following a stable rhythmical pattern; (3) habitual behavior or the facts of associative memory; (4) practical intelligence as the organically bound capacity of choosing; and (5) spirit.

The first level of biopsychic force needs more detailed attention insofar as it plays a major role in understanding spirit. Emotional impulse is the basic force of *all* forms of life (from a protoplasm to human life). Its states are "a mere 'towards,' for example towards light, and 'away from,' and pleasure and pain that are not directed to objects,"[31] and it does not include any reflective information sent to a center.[32] It represents the *unity* of the multiplicity of drives and affects and is the subject of the primary sense of *resis-*

*tance*. Scheler develops this sense of resistance as the root of any having of "reality" (*Wirklichkeit*).[33]

All levels of the biopsychical world belonging to the vital sphere (i.e., all except the spirit) have this in common that they emerge from psychophysical states and remain within the limits of the environment (*Umwelt*). The structure of the environment differs for different organisms insofar as it fits to the specific psychophysical organization or needs of an organism. The environment is an aspect of the world that is relevant for the life functions and organs of a living being. It is an aspect of the world entirely mediated by a psychophysical structure. In "Lehre von den drei Tatsachen" Scheler gives the example of a lizard that would immediately react to a rustle by running away but that would not react at all to a gunshot close by.[34] Other examples would be a dog's sense of environment given through his smell or bees reacting to certain colors or our reaction to food when we are very hungry. Different senses correspond to different environments.

The boundaries of this strict interrelatedness of psychophysical structure and environment are only passed beyond by the last stage of the psychic, by the spirit. According to Scheler, with the spirit, a *new principle* of behavior (*Verhalten*) arises that does not depart any more from a psychophysical structure. According to Scheler, the spirit is existentially (*existentiell*) free from what is organic. A spiritual being is free from the environment and open to the world.[35]

As Scheler points out, humans are not only spiritual beings but also have a psychophysical structure which most of the time guides their behavior (when we "live in the body"). It includes our specific senses, hunger, sexual drives, need for security, and so forth. In view of this "double nature" of human beings I would like to examine how Scheler describes the transition from the "vital sphere" (that remains within the boundaries of the environment) to the "spirit."

Scheler says that the transition from being bound to the environment to being open to a world occurs in such a way that "the centers of 'resistance' and reactions of the environment are elevated to '*objects*' and that the 'whatness' [*Sosein*] of the object is grasped."[36] Centers of resistance are points of psychophysical resistance that are formed by interruptions in a continuum of behavior and that demand for a response. Any threat by another animal leads to the formation of a point of resistance, but also hunger, a stone on a path of an animal, weather conditions, and so on. A being that is world-open does not simply react to these points of resistance but has the ability to objectify what causes them. A human being would, for example, not relate to food merely through hunger (where she would react by simply taking the food and eating it) but she would acknowledge the food *as such*, as an object in itself.

The elevation of centers of resistance to objects has the character of a distancing[37] and of a dynamic reversal of the relation of the spiritual being to reality and to itself.[38] Whereas in animal behavior every action starts from a physical state of the nerve system together with instincts, drives, and sensible perceptions, the spirit imposes another principle of behavior. For the spirit the starting point of an action is the "*pure whatness* of a complex of intuitions and representations that is elevated to an object."[39] Then follows a *free inhibition or release* (*Hemmung oder Enthemmung*) of an impulse of desire (*Triebimpuls*) starting from the center of the person.[40] To follow our previous example, this could be a restraint from eating or a consecutive yielding to our desire to eat. The *person* of which Scheler speaks is nothing but the center of (spiritual) acts that cannot be objectified. It is the immediately experienced unity of (spiritual) experience.[41]

The inhibition or release of an impulse of desire then leads to the transformation of a thing's objectivity (*Gegenständlichkeit*). This transformation is experienced as having value in itself and as being definite.[42] In other words, the value of an object is experienced as intrinsic to it and independent from any psychophysical activity.

The act of objectification concerns our own physiological and psychological constitution as well as the psychic experiences and functions.[43] Animals perform a simple response (*Rückmeldung*) to sensual contents. But the spiritual act performs a second level of reflection: *self-consciousness*, which Scheler also describes as a gathering (*Sammlung*). To gather into self-consciousness and to elevate something given to an object, essentially belong together. They occur in a *distancing* from an environment to a world. The gathering into the I that I described earlier as a spatiotemporal differencing from body modifications is one possible way to understand the gathering into self-consciousness in distancing oneself from the body.

According to Scheler, the essential difference between psychophysical being and psychospiritual being is based on separate principles of being. My suspicion is that we can distinguish two principles of being only as a consequence of a differencing that occurs "bodily." Although Scheler does not give to this differencing a more original status than to the two principles of being, his language seems to refer to such a spatiotemporal differencing when he speaks of a "*distancing* of environment to world" when he speaks of an "*elevation*" of centers of resistance and of a complex of intuitions and representations to an object, and finally of an *inhibition* or *release* of drive impulses. The direction of his language clearly goes from the vital to the spiritual.

What, then, allows Scheler to speak of the spirit as a principle of being separate from the psychophysical being? To understand this better, we will examine acts that are specifically spiritual. Scheler speaks of "acts of ideation" (*Akte der Ideierung*) as acts that go beyond the limits of our sensible experience and that are valid not only for the actually existing world but for all possible worlds.[44] In order to achieve an act of ideation, the real character (*Wirk-lichkeitscharakter*) of things and world must be suspended. These acts presuppose the strict separation of essence and existence. Scheler gives several examples: If I suffer pain in my arm and start questioning what pain is in itself and why there is pain at all in the world, then I perform an idealizing act. Likewise Descartes questions the essential nature of bodies by using the example of a piece of wax. Acts of idealization take single examples and separate them entirely from reality in order to think essences as such.[45]

At this point a question arises: What lets us perform this separation from reality? Where does it come from? Scheler's answer is: spirit.

To use an expression of Scheler, the spirit as the essence of humans is performed in such a way that a powerful NO is thrown against reality.[46] Our sense of reality is given by the experience of resistances that is rooted, as we already heard, in the most basic level of life. Scheler refers to this basic level also as impulse or urge (*Drang*).[47] Insofar as it is the basic level of psychic being, it precedes all consciousness, all representation, and all perception.[48] Nevertheless drive impulses cannot account for the no that is thrown against itself. Here Scheler differs essentially from Nietzsche who attributes the negation of life (nihilism) to drives and instincts—that is, to life itself.[49]

In Nietzschean terms, Scheler's description of the activity of spirit perfectly describes nihilism. In fact Scheler writes that to idealize the world means "to attempt to *dissolve* [*aufheben*] (for us) the *moment of reality itself*, to annihilate that whole, inseparable impression of reality with its affective correlate—it means to remove that 'earthly anxiety.'"[50] The dissolution of the moment of reality is at the same time the dissolution of the anxiety because the reality that is experienced in a resistance is "an inhibiting, restraining pressure and its correlate is 'pure' anxiety (without object)."[51]

According to Scheler, the emerging of spiritual acts is tied to the idea of God. At the same time that humans objectify the world and themselves in acts of idealization, they "must also grasp the most formal *idea of an infinite and absolute being beyond the world*."[52] Because in the very moment that a human being has objectified and thus separated him/herself from nature, s/he must ask him/herself: "Where do I myself stand?" Turning back upon oneself, one, so to speak, looks into nothingness. And this look into nothingness leads to the metaphysical question: "Why is there *at all* a world, why am 'I' *at all*?"[53] Thus, the understanding of the world, of oneself, and of God, constitute a structural unity.

Spirit and, with spirit, metaphysics arise in the negation of life and in the experience of nothingness. Looking back at the differentiating movement of the gathering into the "I," we can now further explain this spatiotemporal movement as a differencing of nothingness and being. In the very moment that a differencing from bodily motions occurs, that a distancing and separating from our psychophysical embeddedness into an environment takes place, we face nothingness and are brought to question being. If I try to think this spatiotemporal differencing from within my experiencing it, its source remains unknown to me. All consciousness I gain of myself, all reflection on my bodily motions, all objectifying, all questioning of what the principle of this differencing is, occur as its effects. Thus, the two principles of being Scheler finds, namely drive and spirit, appear to be deduced from the effects of the spatiotemporal differencing. They presuppose an act of objectification that is the result of distancing and "elevating" given (not-yet) phenomena to objects of our understanding.

But we would do injustice to Scheler's thinking if we reduced it to a platonic dualism, that is, to a dualism that assumes two separate realms: that of the physical and that of the spiritual. Despite his clear distinction of drive and spirit, Scheler takes considerable steps in understanding their relatedness. In *Man's Place in Nature* he thinks this relatedness even in terms of their mutual "penetration." We also should take into account that the spatiotemporal differencing I discussed indeed implies a difference that does not derive from a primordial unity. Our experience occurs as differencing, separating, and gathering. There is no way I can go behind my experience and find a unitary source. There also remains the fact that we do experience a "suspension," an alienation from our bodily embeddedness in our environment when we start asking metaphysical questions, and we do not know the source of this suspension. There is no way we can reduce one way of being to the other (being embodied in an environment and asking metaphysical questions).

## d.   The Mutual Penetration of Life and Spirit

As stated earlier, according to Scheler, the spirit can inhibit or release drive impulses. In doing so, the spirit does not simply eliminate these impulses, but rather transforms them. In *Man's Place in Nature*, Scheler thinks that the spirit receives its energy from repressed drive energy.[54] So, together with a "de-realization" (*Entwirklichung*) of drive impulses, spirit realizes itself. The activity of the spirit, the love, will, spiritual wondering, or despair that might be experienced in what Scheler calls a spiritual act, all draw their "life" from repressed drive impulses such as sexual drive, hunger, and drive to live.

At this point, Scheler sees the danger of reducing the spirit to its origin from repressed drive impulses. He counters this danger with a "claim" and "conviction":

According to my conviction that negative activity, that "no" to reality, that abolishing, inactivating, of the drive-centers that give reality and images, *does not* condition *the being of the spirit* but only, so to speak, its *supply with energy* and thus *its ability to manifest itself.* [. . .] Spirit as such, in its "pure" form, is *originally completely without any "power," "force," "activity."* In order to have a slightest degree of force and activity, that *asceticism,* that repression and at the same time *sublimation* of drives must be *added.*[55]

Scheler's late theory of the "powerlessness" of the spirit moves a considerable step toward uniting two principles that otherwise would be too far apart for any "living" thinking to occur. Remarkably, what Scheler thinks to be "goal and end of all mortal being and occurring," is the *"spiritualization of drives"* and the *"enlivening of the spirit."*[56] But if this thinking of the powerlessness of the spirit is viewed in itself, it appears problematic with respect to Scheler's own phenomenology. Scheler claims that the spirit cannot be objectified, that it can only be experienced in participating in a spiritual act. Therefore, the only way in which I can have knowledge of the spirit is in its activity. But at the same time this activity is understood to be a sublimation of basic drives, drives that are blind for ideas, forms, shapes, drives that have no specific direction, in other words, drives that are in themselves chaos.[57] How, then, can we understand spirit "purely"? For instance, a main determination Scheler gives of the spirit is love. He understands love to be a tendency to go beyond itself. How could we possibly understand this love independently from all force and activity? Is not a spirit without power a spirit without any property? Does not the thought of a spirit in itself, outside any manifestation, evaporate into its own nothingness?

e.   Conclusion

Scheler's phenomenology of the body moves largely in a Christian-platonic tradition insofar as he presupposes two opposed principles of being—spirit and drive—and insofar as he clearly values the spirit more highly than the body. But within this Christian-platonic setting there are openings, gaps, incongruities, that move beyond it and open new possibilities to think "body" and the role bodily motions play in thinking. These openings can be found in the way Scheler thinks rather than in what he explicitly states.

In conceiving the body (which he thinks as a psychophysical phenomenon that can be articulated in interior and exterior experience) as an analyzer that selects and determines (but does not produce) the content of our consciousness, possibilities are opened to consider much more carefully the psychophysical constituents of thinking. By paying closer attention to bodily motions accompanying certain thoughts, we might start to discover a multiplicity of "interests," of drives and impulses that codetermine what we think.

Within what might appear to be simple thoughts we might discover desire for power, dominance, anxiety, and "blind" impulses that have a complex history inscribed in our bodies and in our bodily relation to the world. This does not necessarily imply that we reduce what we think to perceivable bodily motions.

Further, Scheler's account of idealizing acts, the way he describes the transition from the psychophysical embededness in an environment to a spiritual attitude toward the world touches an originating event of thinking as we experience it in the very occurrence of thinking. I described this event as a spatiotemporal differencing that occurs as a differencing from nothingness and being.[58] This differencing leads to a distancing from body motions and from the environment and to an elevation of given phenomena to objects of thought. In this way also, the body becomes an object of Scheler's thought. However, we saw how this spatiotemporal differencing may be conceived as the opening of the bodily dimension of thought, which entails, of course, that "bodily" be not understood merely in relation to kinesthetic body motions.

Finally, in describing the task of human being as the "spiritualization of drives" and the "enlivening of the spirit," Scheler moves toward an overcoming of a hierarchical understanding of "body" (the psychophysical world) and spirit, thus moving toward what seems to be a main interest of contemporary continental philosophy: to bring lived experience into thinking or to ground thinking into life.

*Chapter Four*

# Thinking in the Flesh
## Merleau-Ponty's *The Visible and the Invisible*

Merleau-Ponty's thought appears to take a direction that is very much opposed to what the last chapter revealed about Scheler. Where Scheler sees the psychophysical sphere as a stepping stone to higher acts of thought that arise precisely in the sublimating negation or repulsion of the psychophysical sphere of being, Merleau-Ponty wants to tie thinking back to the field of experiences in which it first arises. Where for Scheler acts of ideation reveal the true essences of things, for Merleau-Ponty these acts lose the true nature of things that cannot be found in abstract essences but only in the intimate awareness of our opaque and dense bodily entanglement with them.

Despite these differences there are also moments of thought in which Scheler and Merleau-Ponty are very close. Both see the body as a major constitutive of and organizing factor in our entanglement with the world, and Scheler's conception of the body as an analyzer that determines if and how we perceive something can be found in similar ways in Merleau-Ponty's *Phenomenology of Perception*.[1] Further, Scheler's thought of the mutual penetration of life and spirit leads to a quite "physical" understanding of "spiritual" acts, which is close to Merleau-Ponty's thought that ideas belong to the flesh. But, of course, Scheler's point is to spiritualize drives, to enliven the spirit, and not to lead thinking back to the psychophysical dimension in and as which it arises.

For Merleau-Ponty, then, the task of philosophy is to think without losing touch with what he calls "primitive Being." This primitive Being has a "texture" to it, a depth and "corporeality" that is not simply "matter," and he calls it flesh. Thinking arises in it and may either develop in such a way that it forgets its origins or in a way that brings to thought and language its natal bond with the world. The latter marks Merleau-Ponty's own attempt, an attempt that is very much akin to the concern of the present book.

The present chapter focuses on the project and work in which Merleau-Ponty is most successful in his attempt to articulate the bodily Being in which thinking arises, namely *The Visible and the Invisible*.[2] In this work and the working notes that go along with it, Merleau-Ponty abandons the language of consciousness that infuses his earlier work *Phenomenology of Perception* and departs more radically from an articulation of perception in terms of a relationship between a perceiving subject (consciousness) and a world with perceived things (objects).

He thinks the body neither in terms of an object nor simply subjectively but rather as flesh that emerges in the flesh of the world. As we will see, with "flesh" Merleau-Ponty attempts to think the "sensibility" of Being not simply in terms of crude matter but as encompassing the invisible dimensions that belong to it. He calls it an "element" "in the sense of a general thing, midway between the spatiotemporal individual and the idea, a sort of incarnate principle."[3] The flesh of the world is saturated with meaning. This is why it is possible for thought and ideas to emerge from this flesh and, in turn, they carry meaning only insofar as they are sensible. In *The Visible and the Invisible* Merleau-Ponty calls this bond between flesh and ideas "the most difficult point."[4] It is precisely this point we need to address in our quest to think the bodily dimension in thought and the belonging of this thought to the brute world in which it originates.

a.   Re-flecting Primitive Being

The "brute world" designates the world that we originally experience insofar as we share its flesh. It is the world the sense of which is revealed to us in our bodily being in the world prior to any explicit thought, the world that is not yet objectified in thinking. The issue is to think and articulate this brute world and with it primitive Being without objectifying it, and to investigate our bodily Being in this world from within this nonobjectified being.

The main obstacle that Merleau-Ponty encounters in this investigation is the very means by which we are used to conduct it: the way thinking occurs reflectively. This is why he begins *The Visible and the Invisible* with a critique of traditional reflexive thought. Merleau-Ponty is especially critical with respect to the traditional philosophical reflection that, as he says, transposes the incarnated subject into a transcendental subject and the reality of the world into an ideality,[5] thus losing touch with the "natal bond with the world."[6] Here Merleau-Ponty probably has in mind Kant and Husserl who, although certainly in quite different ways, think of the relation to the world and to things by reflecting on the way in which what is thought is constituted by or in the thinking subject.[7] Thus, reflection articulates itself in terms of a subject-object relation that loses the "natal bond"—its origination in the "primitive" world that may be originally experienced in prereflexive bodily perception. Such traditional reflection seems to be doomed to fail what it attempts to reach, namely its own originating event and the world in which it arises.[8]

And yet it seems that there would be no philosophy without a kind of reflection, without a kind of bending back of thinking on itself, since it is precisely in this bending back that philosophy attempts to understand beings as such as well as the relation of thinking to itself and to what it reflects. One may question whether there can even be a kind of thoughtful reflection that would not lose touch with its natal bond, a kind of reflection that—as Merleau-Ponty says—"turns back over the density of the world in order to clarify it, but which, [afterwards], reflects back to it only its own light."[9] If so, this reflection would no longer be understood to originate in the thinking subject but rather in the world in which the "subject" is incarnated and it would reflect itself as it originates in the world.

To think "primitive" or "brute" Being (*être primitif, être brut*) "in itself" as it might be prior to all reflection is impossible. Merleau-Ponty is well aware of that. Reflection always already introduces an alteration into the world upon which it reflects because it itself belongs to the world.[10] This can have a number of possible consequences for our understanding of brute Being. One possibility could be to abandon the attempt altogether. Another could be to maintain that since we cannot think brute Being prior to our reflection, this notion is just a construction of thought and does not address what it ought to: actual Being as we experience it in prereflexive perception, and thus the world in which we are incarnated.

These two options place primitive Being in opposition to thinking. Another option would be to think them not as opposed but rather as belonging together. It seems to me that with respect to these options, Merleau-Ponty's position remains ambiguous. If, on the one hand, he writes that the sensible world is much older than the intelligible world,[11] on the other hand, he maintains that different strata of Being, which have traditionally been articulated in terms of an opposition between nature and culture, between the sensible and the intelligible, between the visible and the invisible, cannot be clearly distinguished. This means that these so-called oppositions are no opposition at all. They are same and also not the same. He will eventually articulate such relations in terms of "chiasm."

The proper way, then, to approach brute Being according to Merleau-Ponty would be not an attempt to interrogate it in opposition to thinking but rather to interrogate it as it arises in Merleau-Ponty's thinking and in our engagement with his thinking. This will lead right to the center of the chiasm (the structure of reversibility) that articulates Being and its sensible element: flesh.

For now, we may rephrase the question of how to think brute Being by asking: How can we hold the natal bond with the world as we think?

Merleau-Ponty says that the philosopher "suspends the brute vision only in order to make it pass into the order of the expressed: that vision remains his model or measure, and it is upon that vision that the network of significations which philosophy organizes in order to reconquer it must open."[12] Here, Merleau-Ponty speaks of different orders: Thinking suspends the prereflexive[13] engagement with things in order to transpose it to the order of the expressed. In this suspension, the prereflexive bodily engagement is not lost but remains the "natal soil" and measure for that transposition. However, it is not to be taken for granted that thinking takes prereflexive lived experience as measure for its thinking. Indeed, in traditional philosophical reflection this lived measure gets lost. In order to maintain contact in our thought with primitive Being what we need—according to Merleau-Ponty—is "a sort of *sur-réflexion* (Lingis translates it as *hyperreflection*) that would also take itself and the changes it introduces into the spectacle into account."[14]

In the passage from which this quotation is drawn, Merleau-Ponty gives only a few indications that may elucidate more this sur-réflexion (hyperreflection). He says, for instance, that it would not cut the "organic bonds of perception and perceived thing." This means that it is a reflection that does not objectify its own occurrence as traditional philosophical reflection does. In objectifying itself it would lose touch with the "organic bonds" of the sensible Being that is disclosed in bodily perception.

This nonobjectifying hyperreflection is a reflexive awareness that lets be occurrences that are opened up in it. Such awareness for instance is required in the performing arts (in fact, I suspect that it is at play in any conscious activity that implies a truly creative moment). I may find this reflexive awareness in certain moments in dancing or making music where I find myself aware in the event of the dance or the event of music that seems to occur in a strange way beyond my control, events in which I find myself not as an agent but rather as an absorbed as well as perceptive spectator. This awareness is like witnessing an event where the witness is not just absorbed into an activity but also has a distance to it. And yet this witnessing awareness is not merely passive but allows through its occurrence an opening, a coming into light of an event which otherwise would remain obscured or would not happen at all.

With respect to thinking primitive Being, this awareness (or what Merleau-Ponty calls hyperreflection) occurs such that it continues to bear witness to the bodily being in the world by keeping it manifest in events of thought and articulation. This awareness or hyperreflection also witnesses the losses that occur in moments of reflection and at the same time witnesses the arising of words, images, and configurations of bodies. It would include not only the play of senses and shifting perceptions (for example, how my eyes move as they glide on things in shifting perspectives, sounds that arise and fade away) but would also include awareness of other dynamic dimensions of thinking, like shifts of moods, resistances, openings, closures, tensions, and other bodily motions.

Such reflexive awareness occurs in articulations that do not necessarily involve speech. Rather, it remains mostly silent, without words. And this brings us back to another indication that Merleau-Ponty gives in the quoted passage of *The Visible and the Invisible* concerning hyperreflection. He says that this kind of reflection would allow us to express "our mute contact with the things, when they are not yet things said."[15] Our mute contact with things refers to a prereflective and also prelinguistic bodily engagement with things; that is, to a brute perception that, although it lacks articulation through speech, does not lack an articulation that occurs at the level of sense perception (for instance in constellations of bodies, movements, forces).[16]

We approach here one of the most problematic aspects in Merleau-Ponty's thought, namely the question of language and expression. I will deal with this question more extensively toward the end of this chapter. For now I just would like to point out a few things. The problem of expression is notably one of the main incentives that brought Merleau-Ponty to the project of *The Visible and the Invisible*. It has to do with the question of the transposition of the silent sense of the sensible world of perception into the order of expression in thinking (a transposition that occurs in reflection). Even though the two orders are inseparable, there remains a differential gap between them, a gap that Merleau-Ponty thinks at the same time as their jointure.

To express our mute contact with things in language does not mean, for Merleau-Ponty, that language has the power to coincide with a pure silent world. He says, "if we dream of finding again a natural world or time through coincidence [...] then language is a power of error, since it cuts the continuous tissue that joints us vitally to the things and to the past."[17] But instead of understanding language as a mask over Being that interrupts a pure relation to Being, Merleau-Ponty understands it as an expression of Being, or as one among other possible articulations of Being. He says that "we need only to take language too in the living or nascent state, with all its references, those behind it, which connects it to the mute things it interpellates, and those it sends before itself and which make up the world of things said."[18] Language, understood as such an original expression, never coincides with a pure Being but nevertheless carries the silent sense of Beings.[19]

In our interest in reflecting primitive Being, then, and in following Merleau-Ponty's reflections in *The Visible and the Invisible*, we can try to stay alert to the ways in which, if at all, his language reflects a mute contact with things. In this attempt we may also be alert to ways in which his own language operates against his expressed purpose of not thinking in terms of an opposition between perception and world or perception and things, between an original substratum called "brute world" and a superstratum called "intelligible world," oppositions that obscure and limit the silent contact with things.

Merleau-Ponty clearly felt a danger of reducing phenomenology to a linguistic field that would operate only at the level of the already said and loose touch with prereflexive and prelinguistic being in the world. He points repeatedly to perceptual experience and to the possibility of perceiving the "*sous-entendu*"—what is implicitly meant. But nevertheless, in reading him, we also need to be alert—in a kind of "hyperreflection"—to the alterations that language introduces into perception and into his and our understanding of the Being of beings. While remaining attentive to this question of language, the following sections will explore how Merleau-Ponty articulates our originary being-in-the-world.

b.   The Archetype of Perception: Body and Things

In order to articulate the primary experience through which we gain access to the brute world, in *The Visible and the Invisible* Merleau-Ponty makes recourse to the notion of "perceptual faith":

> For us, the "perceptual faith" includes everything that is given to the natural man in the original in an experience-source, with the force of what is inaugural and present in person, according to a view that for him is ultimate and could not conceivably be more perfect or closer—whether we are considering things perceived in the ordinary sense of the word, or his initiation into the past, the imaginary, language, the predicative truth of science, works of art, the others, or history. We are not prejudging the relations that may exist between these different "layers," nor even that they are "layers"; and it is a part of our task to decide this, in terms of what questioning our brute or wild experience will have taught us.[20]

The faith of which Merleau-Ponty speaks here does precisely not require a specific act of consciousness; he even calls it "animal faith"[21]—a faith that is "animal-like"—which we could characterize as being nonthetic (not explicitly positing a being as such) and as occurring in sense perception. Accordingly, Merleau-Ponty does not understand the perception it involves as a perception that would lead to a conscious objectivation of what one perceives in correlation to a perceiving subject. However perceptual faith reveals to us not only our basic experience of the world, of being in the world and our silent connection with things, but also the way we reach into the past, the imaginary, and ideas, which are areas that imply, if one may say so, quite sophisticated modes of expression. In this context Merleau-Ponty almost speaks of different layers (*couches*)[22] but then puts the adequacy of this word into question. Instead he will characterize the originary "natural" experience of perception that is at play in perceptual faith as an archetype that is originarily at play in all different kinds of encounter with the past, the imaginary, and with ideas: "Perception as an encounter with natural things," he writes, is "the archetype of the originating encounter, instituted and renewed in the encounter with the past, the imaginary, the idea."[23]

The archetype of perception is not a basis that is always present and on which other layers of perception and thinking would occasionally build, but rather it is an archetype in the sense that also in the act of imagination or in thinking of an idea it is originarily at play (it is renewed). This suggests that if we understand this archetype of perception we will have a key to understand all possible original modes of relating to things (in the largest sense of the word) or of being in the world.

What happens, then, in our natural encounter with things?

Here we are not in the position of a *kosmotheoros*, as Merleau-Ponty calls it, whose "sovereign gaze finds the things each in its own time, in its own place";[24] we do not look at things as being in front of us, but rather find ourselves in the perceived, enveloped by it. The act of perception dissolves into the perceived, or, to be more precise, the act of perception and with it our body appears to first emerge *from* the perceived.[25] According to Merleau-Ponty we are united with things through our body and the body emerges as a being from the texture of things by differentiation:

> The body unites us directly with the things through its own ontogenesis, by welding to one another the two outlines of which it is made, its two laps: the sensible mass it is and the mass of the sensible wherein it is born by segregation and upon which, as seer, it remains open.[26]

He gives a description of how this occurs, a description that attempts to transpose into language our pretheoretical perception of things by questioning the "experience-source" of perception:

> What makes the weight, the thickness, the flesh of each color, of each sound, of each tactile texture, of the present, and of the world is the fact that he who grasps them feels himself emerge from them by a sort of coiling up or redoubling, fundamentally homogeneous with them; he feels

that he is the sensible itself coming to itself and that in return the sensible is in his eyes as it were his double or an extension of his own flesh.[27]

The perceiver "feels," finds himself homogeneous with the sensible qualities of things (and here Merleau-Ponty mentions not only touch and vision as in other occasions, but also sound), he finds himself emerging from them in a coiling movement or redoubling, and in this movement of coming to himself as sensible, he experiences the sensible of things as an extension of his own flesh.[28]

In this last part of Merleau-Ponty's description there is a shift in the directionality of thought from the emerging coming-to-himself of the perceiver to his experience that what he perceives is an extension of himself. Merleau-Ponty does not say that in coming to himself the perceiver experiences himself as an extension of the flesh of things in which he was immersed. Rather the flesh of things is now experienced as an extension of the perceiver's own flesh, so that the perceiver comes to be primary with respect to the perceived.

Merleau-Ponty's description continues as follows:

> The space, the time of the things are shreds of himself, of his own spatialization, of his own temporalization, are no longer a multiplicity of individuals synchronically and diachronically distributed, but a relief of the simultaneous and of the successive, a spatial and temporal pulp where the individuals are formed by differentiation.[29]

This latter part suggests that not only the space and time of things but also the perceiver's spatialization and temporalization are formed in this process of differentiation.[30]

Merleau-Ponty's shift in perspectives in the description of our primordial encounter with things reflects the fact that for him there is no fusion between the visible and one's vision, between perceiving and perceived (*percipere* and *percipi*). The two are simultaneous, "the world and I are within one another."[31] Merleau-Ponty often speaks of encroachment or intertwinement. And yet, the world and my body are not one. He articulates this encroachment also as the chiasm of the flesh of the body and the flesh of the world. The sensible dimension of the encroachment (the element within which and as which the encroachment occurs) is, as he says, the same. He calls it flesh, we may also say Being experienced and understood in its sensibility. But the flesh of the body and the flesh of the world remain at the same time different. Merleau-Ponty again articulates their intertwinement in its two perspectives. On the one hand, he says that our flesh (our body) "lines and envelops all the visible and tangible things," on the other hand, "each landscape of my life [...] [is] a segment of the durable flesh of the world."[32]

Before considering further how this double articulation emerges we may consider the relation between the notions of perception, flesh, body, things, and world while remaining mindful of the experience-source of body and things that Merleau-Ponty considers as an archetype of our relation to the world in all its variations.

Merleau-Ponty describes the flesh of the body as "the coiling over of the visible upon the seeing body, of the tangible upon the touching body."[33] The flesh of the body is experienced when in perception the perceiver finds herself emerging and coiling on herself from the perceptions (percipi) of things in their sensible qualities. He calls this coming to herself of the perceiver a movement of temporalizing and spatializing. Thus the flesh of the body names the ontological dimension of the body as it emerges in and out of the intertwinings with things, and subsequently body finds a double determination as perceiving and perceived.

The flesh of the world, as Merleau-Ponty considers it in a working note of 1960 ("Flesh of the world—Flesh of the body—Being"), also has a spatial, temporal, and dynamic determination. As this note suggests, in its temporal quality the flesh of the world is "segregation" (which occurs through differentiation), in its spatial quality it is "dimension," and in its dynamic quality it is "continuation, latency, encroachment."[34] In the Visible and the Invisible he says the flesh, understood as an element, is "inauguration of the where and when," it is "facticity."[35] Thus the time and space of things that Merleau-Ponty describes as "a spatial and temporal pulp where the individuals are formed by differentiation"[36] name the flesh of the world. The flesh of the world is that event of Being in which by virtue of differentiation (segregation) things are formed, one may also say, take place. From the perspective of perceiving, things are not "in themselves, in their own place, in their own time; they exist only at the end of those rays of spatiality and of temporality emitted in the secrecy of my flesh."[37]

Merleau-Ponty's account of the encroachment of the flesh of the body and the flesh of the world appears not to allow a centering of perception in a human subject: the body is experienced as being of the flesh of the world as much as things in their happening are thought and experienced to be extensions of the body. The two are reversible. However, despite the fact that he says that the flesh of the body cannot explain the flesh of the world,[38] Merleau-Ponty considers the relation of the body to itself as perceived as a measure for all other perceived things,[39] so that the body's self-relation appears to be an archetype of the body's relation to things—an archetype of the archetype of perception that reveals to us the flesh of the world.

## c.   Recoiling Flesh and the Genesis of Perception

Merleau-Ponty says that the flesh that he conceives as "the coiling over of the visible upon the seeing body, of the tangible upon the touching body," is "*attested* [my emphasis] in particular when the body sees itself, touches itself seeing and touching the things, such that, simultaneously, *as* tangible it descends among them, *as* touching it dominates them all and draws this relationship and even this double relationship from itself, by dehiscence or fission of its own mass."[40] In another passage he says that there is no fusion between flesh of the world and flesh of myself "*because* [my emphasis] between my body looked at and my body looking, by body touched and my body touching, there is overlapping and encroachment, so that we must say that the things pass into us as well as we into the things."[41]

Merleau-Ponty says that we can experience and think the difference between and intertwinement of perceiving and perceived, of flesh of the body and flesh of the world because we find this difference within our own body.

From this one could draw two quite different conclusions. The first would be that Merleau-Ponty still remains caught in a subjective thought, in fact in a kind of narcissism, since the relation to the world is derived from a relation to oneself.[42] The other to oneself is assimilated by being seen as the other *of* oneself. The second conclusion one could draw is that the body, conceived as the medium of experience and thought of myself, things, and world, is not quite "mine" but is as much of the world (in fact, Merleau-Ponty says that it belongs to the flesh of the world) as it is constitutive of "me" as a site and act of perception. A "dehiscence," says Merleau-Ponty, "opens my body in two." If this dehiscence marks the site of difference, or, to be more precise, of differentiation between percipere and percipi, between things and my body, then the body becomes a site of radical differences, or rather of differentiations that disrupt a subjective understanding of it. We should therefore differentiate a body in a more narrow sense—that is, the body as perceiving in its difference to things and world—from the body in a larger sense, conceived as the site of articulation of I, others, things, world, in their encroachment.

Of the two conclusions just mentioned I will try to follow the path of the second, since it leads to a more radical reading of Merleau-Ponty. The doubling of the body into phenomenal body and objective body, in which the objective body belongs to the perceived world, evokes the image of two layers of the body, but in this respect Merleau-Ponty corrects himself:

One should not even say, as we did a moment ago, that the body is made up of two leaves, of which the one, that of the "sensible," is bound up with the rest of the world. There are not in it two leaves or two layers; fundamentally it is neither thing seen only nor seer only, it is Visibility sometimes wandering sometimes reassembled.[43]

Here, like in other passages, Merleau-Ponty works at blurring conceptions and images of distinct "things" (body, things, world) that would enter into a relationship with each other. The body, like all "things," is fundamentally open and opaque. "Where are we to put the limit between the body and the world, since the world is flesh?" Merleau-Ponty asks himself at some point.[44] One cannot set such a limit "objectively" or "definitively." This limit remains dynamic. To understand it one needs to turn back to the ontogenesis of the body and articulate it as it is experienced in its origination, when it is not yet conceived as thing.

We saw how Merleau-Ponty does this in the passage where he describes the body emerging from the texture (flesh) of things and as subsequently experiencing this texture as an extension of itself. By trying to stay aware—in a hyperreflection—of the alterations that thought introduces in the experience of brute Being I pointed to a shift in the directionality of Merleau-Ponty's thought in that passage. First he describes the perceiver's coming to herself as sensible, and then the perceiver experiences that from which she first emerged as an extension of her own flesh. How are we to interpret these alterations of thought?

Merleau-Ponty's description of the emerging of body in its differentiation from things coincides with a movement of thought, a coming to awareness of a relation with/to things and others. He suggests how we should understand thinking in relation to the recoiling of flesh in a working note of September 1959 where he says: "every reflection is after the model of the reflection of the hand touching by the hand touched."[45] *Every* reflection, and this means also a nonobjectifying awareness or what Merleau-Ponty calls hyperreflection, follows the model of the touching-touched hands. The model that Merleau-Ponty takes from Husserl is well known. When I touch with my left hand my right hand as my right hand is touching something else, lets say an apple, I perceive my right hand either as being touched by my left hand or as touching the apple, but never as both at once, even if both happens at once. Likewise, when my two hands touch each other I cannot perceive one hand as touching and being touched at once. Between touching and being touched there is reversibility, but this reversibility is never completed, that is, there is no coincidence between touching and being touched.[46]

Now how are we to understand *any* form of reflection according to his model? It certainly works with the earlier account of how I emerge from being absorbed into the texture of things. Let's say I see an ice cube; at first I "am" (in) the sensing of its cool, transparent surface, imagining how it would melt between my fingers or on my tongue; then I "come to myself," I am aware that I am looking at the ice cube and am aware of my fantasies of touch and taste, and, still in the reverberations of having been absorbed into these sensations and images, I experience that ice cube in its temporal, sensible Being as an extension of my flesh. When I reflect on my perception of the ice cube my perspective shifts and the ice cube becomes an "other" with respect to my act of perception. I am loosing that state of absorption into the hard, cool, melting surface of the cube. A hyperreflection is what allows me to trace the shift from absorption to self-awareness, to acknowledge the hiatus in that shift and to retain the reverberation of the prior absorption that allows me to see the "two" states as being the articulation of one event. The recoiling of my body out of its absorption in things to the awareness of perception and the experience of the texture of things as extensions of my perceiving coincides with the movement of reflection. Flesh is the element that extends in the recoiling and thus inaugurates a "when" and "where." Reflection is the movement of differentiation that characterizes flesh.

In fact, does not what Merleau-Ponty calls a "model" for all reflection, the touching-touched hands, already describe a reflection of thought? Does it not, further, describe a reflexive act that moves toward a traditional differentiation between subject and object in its distinction between a *percipere* and a *percipi*? Yes, one should say, but precisely because the model of reflection moves *toward* a differentiation of perceiving subject and perceived object says that it does not move *from* such a differentiation, it does not posit it at the outset. Thus, Merleau-Ponty appears to succeed in a way of thinking that is *not yet* differentiated into subject and object and that thus keeps the natal bond with the "brute Being" in which it arises.

However, beyond articulating thought as occurring after the model of the touching-touched hands, Merleau-Ponty claims that the reversibility it articulates is not proper to thought first and above all, but to the flesh of the world, to the texture of Being. For this we may try to get closer to the birthplace of perception, to where *percipere* and *percipi* are not yet differentiated. This birthplace, Merleau-Ponty tells us, is not coincidence. In fact, at the core of the reversibility that articulates perception we find a gap, a "point zero." This gap coincides with the dehiscence that, as he says, opens my body in two.

d.   The Negative Opening of Intercorporeal Being

The gap at the core of the chiasm is a point of differentiation between what comes to be articulated as "body and things," "I and world," and "I and others." The last was omitted in our previous analyses even though Merleau-Ponty refers to the issue of the "other" early on in his text. However the other is omitted in Merleau-Ponty's model of reflection and we followed a certain procedure suggested by Merleau-Ponty's work that moves from a reductive account of reversibility (in the touching-touched body) to its more complex structure.[47]

The other is essentially at play in every actual perception. To perceive a natural thing implies not only the awareness of my perception but also of the fact that others perceive the same thing. To reflect on myself implies that I am aware of my being for others. In fact, Merleau-Ponty comes up with the same four-term system that we find in Sartre's *Being and Nothingness*: "my being for me, my being for the other, the for itself of the other, and his being for me."[48] One should note, however, that whereas for Sartre this four-term system constitutes human existence, for Merleau-Ponty it articulates the opening of a world in which I, others, things, and world first come to be in chiasmic relations. It names the intersection where an intercorporeal world opens.

This point of intersection is the initial opening, the "zero of Being" that we need to keep in mind in order to think from "within" the world (brute Being) and not by objectifying it. Merleau-Ponty reflects on this "point zero" especially in his latest working notes. In June 1960 he writes:

Show that philosophy as interrogation [. . .] can consist only in showing how the world is articulated starting from a zero of Being which is not nothingness, that is, in installing itself on the edge of Being, neither in the for Itself, nor in the in Itself, at the joints, where the multiple *entries* of the world cross.[49]

In saying that the "zero of Being," the "joints" (note the plural) from where an articulation into for itself and in itself, into body and things in the world, and so on, occurs, is not nothingness, Merleau-Ponty says that the gap at the center of reversibility or reflection is not a negativity as opposed to positively stated beings.[50] At the zero of Being, multiple entries of the world cross; it is rather a point of opening and closing articulation than of a not-being. It also is a point that occurs in the middle of articulations of beings. Further, there is not just one point zero, one joint, but a multiplicity of articulating openings.

This note of Merleau-Ponty seems to me to be faithful to the event of reversibility as I would reflect it in a hyperreflection. In directing my awareness to a motion of reflection I find myself always already in the middle of particular events of articulation. At the same time, the opening of those articulations escapes my grasp, it withdraws as it gives articulation to what "I" then reflect as beings or perceive as visible: my body, things in the world, others, my body as touching, seeing, or as being touched, seen, and so on.

The for itself and in itself is one possible articulation that I reflect as belonging together by virtue of the articulating opening of a world that "I" may witness. This is why Merleau-Ponty can say in another note that: "In reality there is neither me nor the other as positive, [as] positive subjectivities. There [they] are two caverns, two opennesses, two stages where something will take place—and which both belong to the same world, to the stage of Being."[51] This implies that the "I" of which I speak in saying that I am aware or reflect something, is not there at the outset, but is itself the result of a reflection of an articulation that comes to be in the crossing with the other as they open in articulating junctures that are in themselves no thing—nothing.

In April 1960, Merleau-Ponty writes:

> The primary I [. . .] is the unknown *to whom* all is given to see or to think, to whom everything appeals, before whom . . . there is something. It is therefore negativity—ungraspable in person, of course, since it is *nothing*."[52]

But who is it, then, Merleau-Ponty asks, who thinks, talks, argues, suffers, and enjoys? He answers by saying that the "who" is "this negativity as openness, by the body, to the world."[53] The negativity of which Merleau-Ponty speaks here is that point zero, those jointures he named in the other note, and the openness *to* the world suggests the articulating opening of a world that occurs, as he says now, through [par] the body. Continuing that thought he says: "Reflexivity must be understood by the body, by the relation to [it] self of the body, of speech. [. . .] The body-negative or language-negative duality *is* the subject.[54]

Here also the question of language and thus of expression reappears. But before turning to it, I would like to dwell first on the role body plays in the articulating opening of a world. Body is thought as a negativity through which articulating opening occurs. Or—said the other way around—the opening at which the jointures of the crossing articulations occur, occurs through the body. We arrive here at a further articulation of the body. We saw earlier that the body is not simply either perceiving or perceived; as sensing-sensed it is constituted by a dehiscence. It arises from the flesh of the world in a dehiscence that distances it at the same time. Through this distance the flesh of things (things as they take place in time) is experienced as an extension of the flesh of the body. Beyond these pervious articulations of the body as perceiving-perceived and as "incorporating" a dehiscence, we should now consider the body also in view of others, as Merleau-Ponty says in another note of the same period (April 1960): "One feels oneself looked at (burning neck) not because something passes from the look to our body to burn it at the point seen, but because to feel one's body is also to feel its aspect for the other."[55]

I understand Merleau-Ponty to be speaking here of a bodily awareness akin to "being touched," of a sudden sense of intimate strangeness which calls to be understood or articulated, and to which I find myself responding for instance by turning my body around and finding somebody looking at me, and then maybe by reflecting on the difference between my feeling touched and the other's gaze.[56] In these experiences, my awareness is initiated through a bodily sense of otherness or strangeness at the center of "myself," at the center of a place in which an articulate opening of a situation occurs to me. This sense of otherness precedes my positive acknowledgment of another human being that looks at me as well as my positive acknowledgment of what I come to conceive as myself.

Since in its dehiscence the body, through which I find myself in a world with others and things, incorporates the otherness of other bodies, things, of (as we will see) actual and potential histories and occurrences, strictly speaking "my body" is not mine. That body in which I find myself is at the same time a site and occurrence that keeps me open to otherness, to what can never be called "mine," to what may always remain foreign to "me."

One must say, then, that the "gap" that is opened in the dehiscence of the body and through which I come to find myself in relation to a world, is an opening not only for what positively appears, for sensible, visible things, but also for what does not appear and that Merleau-Ponty calls the invisible.

e.   The Invisible: Ideas of the Flesh

> The "invisible world": it is given originally as *non-Urpräsentierbar*, as the other is in his body *given originally as absent*—as a divergence—as a transcendence.[57]

As this passage from a working note from February 1959 indicates, the invisible world opens with the other. However, this invisible world is not only the world seen by others, as Sartre thinks it;[58] that is, it names not only the perspectives of others, which remain hidden to me. If this were the case, the invisible would be dependent upon other perspectives and would be the collectivity of subjective realms. Yet the invisible names what appears as *Nichturpräsentierbar*— as that which can never become immediately present in itself—in a much wider sense. It is a transcendence that allows things and a world to appear. Further the invisible is not beyond the visible like another realm, but rather it is a dimension *of* the visible, its depth, its Being. It is that negativity that is an opening for the intercorporeal world.[59]

A proper approach to the invisible requires that we think it out of the gap, the negativity that is the initial opening of perception in which emerges the chiasm that articulates perceiving and perceived, I and others, body and world.

We may, at this point, recall the archetype of the originating encounter with things that, as Merleau-Ponty says, is "instituted and renewed in the encounter with past, the imaginary, the idea."[60] These, the past, the imaginary, and the idea are the invisible of the visible. Things that we touch and see are never isolated objects but have an invisible depth to which belong past, the imaginary, and ideas. Since things are perceived (potentially or actually) also by others, the invisible is pregnant with perceptions by others. Things are exposed or open in an intercorporeal, historical world.

We considered earlier how our perception of things occurs in the recoiling of flesh. Out of being immersed in the texture of things we come to find ourselves as our body emerges as perceiving in its encroachment with the perceived thing. This is a spatiotemporal occurrence that marks the time and space of the perceiving body and the perceived things. They take place together in differencing, encroaching upon each other. In this occurrence essence and existence are not separate but the same occurrence. Merleau-Ponty uses Heidegger's notion of *Wesen* (essence understood verbally as occurrence) in order to articulate the indistinction of essence and existence in an originating encounter with things.[61] Wesen is the "existing essence" of things that is not simply the visible but that names the depth of the visible that contains a spatiotemporal dimensionality that transcends the present. He writes: ". . . the visible counts so much for me and has an absolute prestige for me only by reason of this immense latent content of the past, the future, and the elsewhere, which it announces and which it conceals."[62]

The future, past, and elsewhere that belong to the Wesen of things are not projections of the perceiver's temporalizing and spatializing, but are announced by things in her encounter with them, an encounter in which also the perceiver comes to herself. We should add that the invisible dimension of things with their actual and potential histories[63] also announces their exposure to others. At the same time that, in coming to myself, I experience my exposure to others, I also experience the exposure of the things I perceive to others, to perceptions that can never be mine.

All of this: I, a historical world, things, others, open through a dehiscence in my body. In that same gap also thought emerges and ideas are articulated in language.

In fact, Merleau-Ponty describes the negativity at the origin of an articulate opening not only as negative body, but also as negative language. The "negative body" and "negative language" designate the same gap or jointure out of which and in which a world, a site, and time open. And it is only by staying in awareness of this gap that we hold open the sensible dimension of thinking or that thinking originally occurs as an articulation of sensible Being.

But how is it possible that language—the articulation of thought—emerges from the flesh of the world? How can mute, primitive Being be articulated? And how do we account for abstract ideas that do not designate sensible things? We will not be able to answer these questions exhaustively, but in view of the main issue of this book—the bodily dimension in thinking—we may at least get an indication of how Merleau-Ponty would begin to answer these questions.

Ideas belong to the invisible dimension of the world that encompasses, as we saw, others and things with their histories. The idea, says Merleau-Ponty, is "not a *de facto* invisible," "it is the invisible of this world, that which inhabits this world, sustains it, and renders it visible, its own and interior possibility, the Being of this being."[64] Ideas are articulated through language through the body. Merleau-Ponty distinguishes an operative language from a secondary language.[65] The operative language does not simply repeat prior significations but originally names what it signifies. It names the invisible that is given to us in a corporeal experience. Even with reference to ideas expressed in literature and music like the ideas of light or of sound or that of intelligence Merleau-Ponty writes: ". . . the ideas we are speaking of would not be better known to us if we had no body and no sensibility; it is then that they would be inaccessible."[66]

This is the case because the invisible transpires with the visible in the gap that opens for me in the dehiscence of my body. It is through this gap, through this nothingness, that speech may find the operative word to express invisible ideas that are ideas *of* the visible and that at the same time make manifest the visible. However, as noted earlier, language cannot say this invisible directly since words are formed in an articulating difference from the invisible they name.[67]

Merleau-Ponty compares the words that express invisible ideas to the body that in sensing perceives the visible:

> It is as though the visibility that animates the sensible world were to emigrate, not outside of every body, but into another less heavy, more transparent body, as though it were to change flesh, abandoning the flesh of the body for that of language, and thereby would be emancipated but not freed from every condition.[68]

The point of transition from the idea to the operative word is, again, a blind spot. It bears the same structure of reversibility as perceiving and perceived.[69] Only that in the transposition to language the expressed idea is not tied to one perceiving body that operates as a center of articulation.[70] Merleau-Ponty conceives language as being its own body and he claims the same for music.[71] It is thus that words may lose touch with the sensible world in which they arise and operate on a more abstract level. Language is never mine or yours but we participate in it. This also means that it is always shared language; it is implicitly in relation to the other.

### f.  Conclusion

In conclusion I will try to tie together the different threads of this chapter: re-flexivity, body and world, the gap, the visible and the invisible, ideas and language, in order to summarize how Merleau-Ponty thinks the bodily dimension in thinking.

For Merleau-Ponty the task of philosophy is to bring to language brute Being, that is, Being that is not yet objectified in thought. He looks for a way of thinking that may express our originary relation to the world and he looks for this relation in the experience of sense perception. In analyzing acts of sense perception he finds that our body is dynamic and has a texture to it that arises in the world in relation to things. He calls this texture flesh. Flesh is not a static thing but the fundamentally open sensible dimension of things and body that takes place in a recoil of the sensible. This recoil occurs as a spacing and temporalizing of body and things in their differentiation. Thinking, according to Merleau-Ponty, occurs after the model of the touching-touched hands—that is, it occurs as a recoiling differentiation. An analysis of his account of perception showed that the recoiling of flesh is itself a reflection. Thus thinking occurs as the recoiling of flesh. We then followed Merleau-Ponty closer to the source of the recoiling movement that is the gap at the chiasm that finds its articulation in the recoil. The gap is at once point of conversion and radical differentiation. From it emerge body and world, I and other, perceiving and perceived as opposed and reversible terms. This gap is opened in the dehiscence of the body, as Merleau-Ponty calls it, so that the body becomes a site and movement of radical differences.

The gap or negativity at the center of the chiasm of the flesh is also the site of opening to others and the invisible dimension of Being. These are never given directly but obliquely through the visible that emerges in the recoiling of flesh. The invisible dimension of Being is tied to the visible that it sustains. It is the invisible of the visible and comprises its histories, both actually and potentially, the perceptions of others, and ideas. To think these ideas they need to be brought to language. This happens through the same negativity that opens and differentiates through the body perceiving and perceived. One may say that thinking occurs in the recoiling of flesh from an opening that allows the invisible of flesh to come to language.

We find, thus, in Merleau-Ponty a powerful account of the bodily dimension in thinking, an account, of course, that does not claim to make finished statements about the truth in this matter, but that remains tentative and questioning.[72] However it should be clear that for Merleau-Ponty this bodily dimension is not subjective. The body through which thinking occurs is a site of opening of a world and others as much as it is a site where a particular articulation of Being gathers, and an "I" comes to itself and comes to understand itself in relation to an intercorporeal word.

I will end with a few critical remarks, remarks that do not intend to diminish Merleau-Ponty's accomplishments but to delimit places where Merleau-Ponty remains tied to ways of thinking that he seeks to overcome. These delimitations should allow us, then, to see where, together with Merleau-Ponty, one may try to move further in the quest to think without losing the natal bond with sensible Being.

1. According to Merleau-Ponty the failure of our metaphysical tradition to think brute Being is tied to reflexive thought that objectifies the world. This goes along with a primacy of vision.[73] The objectified being is "seen" by the mind. Although the title of Merleau-Ponty's book, The Visible and the Invisible, clearly aims to point to Being's invisible dimension, he seems to repeat the privileging of vision. It is true that he makes reference also to touch and sometimes to hearing, and that in the model of the touching-touched hands visibility seems to emerge from touching, but for him the "visible" often becomes synonymous for things perceived. The primacy of vision influences his account of perception insofar as it moves reflexively into a differentiation of perceiving and perceived. Once the philosopher hyperreflectively gives an account of the perceiver who not only feels himself emerging from the flesh of things but in his recoiling also perceives the perceived as an extension of his body, the philosopher visualizes (presents) in his mind a difference between perceiving and perceived that moves toward an objectification of the perceived in relation to a perceiving subject.

2. One may question whether every perception includes a coming to oneself, or self-awareness, as Merleau-Ponty's description suggests. Most people seem to live most of the time without self-awareness. There are modes of bodily encounter with things, or maybe it would be more accurate to speak of a being with things, where a recoiling differentiation into perceiver and perceived does not happen, as in modes of touching, in listening to music, and in tasting. We may even think of the very common experience of driving a car without being self-conscious about the driving: all of a sudden we "come to ourselves" and realize that we cannot recall the way we just have driven. Would an articulation of such prereflexive modes of Being

not require a description that does not retain as one of its primary differentiating poles the ego?

3.  There also remains the problem that Merleau-Ponty takes as a model of reflection the relation of a body to itself and that he moves from there to the archetype of perception in the encounter of body and things in order then (in the structural order of though) to complicate the structure of reversibility as a four-fold structure that includes the other. Of course Merleau-Ponty would reply that the other is already implicitly present in the model of the touching-touched hands: my hand touched is the other to the touching hand. But is it not the case that the alterity that we find at play in this model is do to the shift in perception? Can we really equate the experience of touching our own hand with the experience of touching the hand of another? Does one not risk to construct again the other as an alter ego—as a double of oneself—thus not thinking the other in her otherness at all? The question is whether one could not find ways of thinking that would initiate reflection at the intersection with for instance animals, institutions, technology, traditions, the other sex (as in fact Irigaray does), and other beings or events that would lead to a quite different articulation of thought.

In summary, what limits Merleau-Ponty is the primacy of perception and with it its articulation into perceiving and perceived. The problem is not only that we are used to understanding perception as a specifically human activity, as something humans do. This understanding is overturned if one carefully reads Merleau-Ponty. In declaring the percipi as more primary than the percipere in the chiasmic articulation of flesh, Merleau-Ponty radically decenters subjectivity. But one may question if one could not go further than the percipi, as in fact Merleau-Ponty does especially in his latest working notes, by focusing on the negativity that is at the same time opening of multiple entries to the world. This opening is not simply a percipi but a more radical articulation of Being. One may say that at this point, Merleau-Ponty breaches beyond phenomenology to a more radical, nonsubjective possibility of thought.

In the next chapters we will look at ways of thinking that radically depart from modes of thinking centered in the subject, although in quite different ways.

# PART THREE

# Exposed Bodies

Although it has been one of my aims to show that the exploration of the bodily dimension in thinking leads to a desubjectivation of thought, among the philosophers that we considered in the previous chapters only Merleau-Ponty explicitly maintains that thinking is of the sensible and that the body reveals to us an intercorporeal world in which also thinking arises. (Nietzsche carries us to that limit but at the same time maintains the impossibility to think the sensible as such.) This requires of course a reconsideration of what we mean by "body" and the "sensible." The body cannot simply designate crude matter or the object of the science, for instance of biology, and the sensible cannot simply mean the matter that physics considers or what we (subjectively speaking) sense with our five senses. Merleau-Ponty takes us beyond that in his considerations of the flesh of the world and of a negativity at the source of perception that is an opening for the sensible and ideas at once. In fact the sensible is sensible in the double sense that it can be sensed and that it makes sense—is meaningful—and the body is revealed in its most originary dimension as a dynamic event of an opening articulation of things and the world.

One may therefore have included Merleau-Ponty under the heading of this third part of the book that considers the bodily dimension in thought as well as determinations of bodies that are not rooted in subjectivity, also because there are moments where Merleau-Ponty's thought in *The Visible and the Invisible* is strikingly close to Heidegger's thought in *Contributions to Philosophy*. However, at the same time Merleau-Ponty remains tied to the phenomenological movement through his privileging of perception. Heidegger would probably have taken this as a sign that Merleau-Ponty is still "metaphysical" and not able to think Being as such from itself. The latter is precisely Heidegger's attempt in *Contributions*. In leaving behind all thinking in terms of transcendence and in the overcoming of the ontological difference, Heidegger attempts to speak out of the event of being without taking any single being (not even Dasein) as intermediary entity to be questioned. He attempts to do what Merleau-Ponty thinks to be impossible: direct ontology.

But this does not mean that Heidegger privileges some kind of disembodied abstract notion of Being. On the contrary, he attempts to think more "concretely," more attuned to experiences of an originary opening of a world, more attuned to the very arising of thought in a historical world. Heidegger is very well aware that there is no event of being without beings. In fact, as he says in *Contributions*, the two occur together (*gleichzeitig*). The issue for him is to think this simultaneity *in* the event of being, which means by not privileging things and a presentational thought that would "objectify" them. The issue, then, is to think beings out of the event of be-ing, that is, from enowning (*vom Ereignis*), as the subtitle of *Contributions* suggests.

Heidegger rarely thematizes the body (Leib) and many contemporary thinkers find that highly suspicious. However, as I will show, *Contributions* opens ways to think the body that are completely consistent with Heidegger's thought. My thesis is that Dasein always occurs bodily and since thinking is a mode of being of Dasein, thinking always occurs bodily. Further, in Heidegger's *Contributions* the notion of Dasein undergoes a transformation; he writes it Da-sein (with a hyphen) and reconceives it not primarily as the being of humans but as the concrete site (time-space) in which a historical world is disclosed. I will show how this leads to an understanding of body as not designating simply the corporeality of humans but the corporeality of the event of be-ing. Consequently, there is a doubling of the notion of body that is similar to the one we find in Merleau-Ponty; body names the body of humans and the site of an opening articulation of a world.

Foucault's understanding of "body" appears to be in a stark contrast to Heidegger's. Heidegger would probably have said that Foucault is a sociologist and historian who thinks representationally (*vorstellungshaft*) and thus fails to see the "true" event of being. But Foucault draws our attention to phenomena and events that shape our bodies and ways of thinking that escape the attention of the philosophers we have so far considered: he writes about institutions and practices that are in turn formed by shifting relations of power that have no subject at their source. Subjects are created and formed through constellations of power. Foucault also challenges the philosophical positions so far considered in that he thinks in singularities of events that cannot be brought into one single "picture." There is no "Being" with a capital "B," nor is there one history of Being one may trace.

Foucault invites us to consider the bodily dimension in thinking "from the outside"—nonreflexively in the traditional sense. This dimension becomes apparent rather through its effects (effects on which of course one must reflect), through what becomes visible to the eye of the historian. But what becomes visible is not a mere surface, even if Foucault and some "Foucaultians" may claim so, but carries reverberations that effect transformations of bodies and thinking. Foucault's descriptions and genealogical accounts make manifest in the visible what escapes the "objective" eye: struggling forces and shifting constellations of power that shape bodies and ways of thinking. Traditional philosophers would have placed these in the "interiority" of their "souls," but Foucault points to how they happen "out there" with us.

In a certain way Heidegger and Foucault approach things from opposed "sides," sides, however, that remain porous to each other if we are attentive to the bodily dimension in thought. Heidegger approaches things "from within" an experience of the event of be-ing, Foucault approaches them "from without." Both approaches are not rooted in a subject, although both approaches take into account the fact that the way of thinking they display is shaped by the very histories they uncover.

That Foucault comes last in my explorations of the bodily dimension in thinking does not mean that he gets the last saying in the matter. But I intend to let the previous explorations be challenged by a limit that poses a limit also to what we are used to call philosophy, this in order to question in the concluding chapter of this book possibilities and limits of what we may call "bodily thinking."

# Chapter Five

# Bodily Being-T/here
## The Question of the Body in the
## Horizon of Heidegger's
## *Contributions to Philosophy*

When in the sixties in one of the seminars of Zollikon[1] somebody asked Heidegger why he wrote so little about the body (Leib),[2] his answer was that the corporeal (*das Leibliche*) is the most difficult question.[3] Indeed we find only few texts where Heidegger speaks explicitly about the body.[4] Before venturing into an exposition of the body and the bodily dimension in Heidegger's thought we should therefore first consider what makes this question so difficult for Heidegger and why he wrote so little about it.

One reason why the question of the body is so difficult for Heidegger certainly resides in our tendency to see the body as an object, a thing, a living thing, certainly, that distinguishes itself from plants and animals insofar as it has a mind. We present (*vorstellen*) the body to our mind as an entity, and presentational thought is exactly what, according to Heidegger, has prevented Western philosophy from asking the more fundamental question of being itself. In fact Heidegger would claim that, if we want to get to the truth of things (and thus also of the body), we would need to ask the question of being itself first.

In *Being and Time* Heidegger opens up the question of being itself precisely by showing that human beings are not entities ("bodies") endowed with reason but Dasein, a word that should let resonate the way we as humans *are*—that is, what characterizes our *being* in a verbal sense. Dasein, literally translated, means being-t/here ("da" in German means both here and there), and for Heidegger the issue is how we *are* t/here. Human *being* is not primarily a being (*ein Seiendes*) but openness to being, not only to our own being and interests but also to the being of beings in general, to the way things are, and to the way in which, for us, a historical world opens. Only because of this openness can we understand beings surrounding us as such. Being as such is a temporal event and it discloses in our being-t/here temporally in a threefold structure (Heidegger speaks of existentials) that characterizes our being-in-the-world: projection, thrownness, and being with things. Only insofar as Dasein projects itself toward the possibilities of its existence into which it is always already thrown does being disclose (*erschließt sich*) and are beings discovered (*entdeckt*) as such.

In *Being and Time* Heidegger notes that even though the projecting-thrown openness to being is more original than what we discover in it, we have a natural tendency to understand ourselves through what is discovered, that is, through the things to which we relate and that we are used to think presentationally.[5] Thus we understand ourselves as beings, as bodies (Körper) with certain faculties, and not from within our openness to being, not from within the temporality that characterizes being.

This tendency remains also when "Heidegger scholars" understand in some way the ontological difference that marks the distinction between the disclosedness of being and the discoveredness of beings, that is, between the temporal event as which being as such is disclosed and our relation to things that come to appear in this temporal event. This tendency is a difficulty that we encounter each time we think. This is true especially of an attempt to think "body." To think being through the ontological difference is certainly one way to keep this difficulty (to think being not as *a* being) open, and Heidegger would always maintain that we need to think through this difference to make a transition from metaphysical thinking (that thinks being—*Sein*—in terms of beings—*Seiendes*) to the thinking of being in itself. But in *Contributions to Philosophy* Heidegger also maintains that the ontological difference, as important as it may be at first for a transition from metaphysics to the thinking of being, becomes a main obstacle to think being in its truth.[6] If we take the ontological difference as a kind of firm structure, we might again fall pray to our natural tendency to understand being in terms of beings by understanding being as a kind of open horizon that transcends beings, an open horizon that analogously to beings would be understood as a higher being beyond beings. By attempting to overcome the ontological difference, in *Contributions* Heidegger has to rethink the difference between be-ing (now written as "Seyn" to mark its temporal character, which Parvis and Maly in their translation of *Contributions* render with the hyphen in be-ing) and beings in a different way, and more explicitly in a way that would more efficiently counter our tendency to think being in terms of beings. But this rethinking of the difference between be-ing and beings also impacts our possibility to think beings, and more specifically the body, more originally from within the opening of the truth of be-ing, without just objectifying them.

In this chapter, I will explore the question of body and the bodily dimension in thinking in the horizon of Heidegger's *Contributions to Philosophy*. I will dedicate the first part of this chapter to a general introduction to the thinking of *Contributions* starting with *Being and Time* and I will then show how Heidegger thinks the difference between be-ing and beings in what he calls be-ing-historical thinking (*seynsgeschichtliches Denken*) in order then to proceed to the more particular question of the body in the second part.[7]

# I. BEING AND BEINGS

a.  From the Thinking of *Being and Time* to that of
    *Contributions*

In the itinerary of Being and Time, the existential analytic of Dasein was supposed to explicate the sense of being of beings in general that Heidegger thinks as original temporality, as a temporal horizon through which the world is disclosed and through which we understand beings as such. Therefore it was required to first explicate the conditions for the possibility of being (the temporality in the sense of the *Zeitlichkeit des Daseins* which in its turn is founded in the *Temporalität des Seins*) in order to then understand beings to which we relate.[8] The question of the different fields of beings as they are represented in our factual life (beings as they are seen and conceived in natural sciences, in sociology, in law, in theology, etc.) would have been a question of the so-called metontology. This would have included also the question of the body and of sexuality.[9]

But Heidegger never developed this metontology. Instead, he interrupted his itinerary of *Being and Time* and performed in the thirties the famous "turn" (*Kehre*) in his thinking that led him to pose again the question of being from a "new beginning." This is not the place to discuss all the implications of this turn. We may recall that Heidegger came to conceive the language of *Being and Time* as inadequate because it encouraged our natural tendency to understand being analogously to beings.[10] Further, he followed the necessity to think being itself in its historicality (*Geschichtlichkeit*). Being is historical insofar as it reveals itself differently in different epochs (ancient Greece, middle ages, modernity) and because it is in itself an occurrence or event (*Geschehen*), the event of the destiny (*Geschick*) of being in different epochs.

Heidegger began to look for a language that would be more originally the language of being in its historicality. This lead to the attempt to project in *Contributions to Philosophy* the fundamental relations (*Grundgefüge*) of the truth of be-ing as *enowning* (*Ereignis*). With the *truth* of be-ing Heidegger designates the movement of simultaneous closure and disclosure in which be-ing occurs: its coming to pass. (Like be-ing, truth has a temporal sense.) With "enowning" Heidegger designates the event of be-ing insofar as it discloses being-t/here and with it humans and gods, earth and world, and beings in a way that lets them shine forth in their differences and belonging together. "Ereignis" in German usually means "event," but Heidegger thinks it also in a more literal sense as the bringing into one's own (*eigenes*) and thus as *"enowning."* The "own" indicates the original dwelling, the historical essence (like be-ing and truth, essence [Wesen], too, has a verbal sense) of what comes to be.

Since the main problem we face here with respect to Heidegger's thought is to think the body out of being itself (conceived temporally as an event of disclosure), we first need to open an access to the thought of be-ing. The main difficulty in this respect is that in order to think being in itself, thinking continuously needs to strive against its natural tendency to comprehend it analogously to beings. A fundamental way to counter this tendency is to hold on to those moments when our natural relation to things remains suspended, alienated (*befremdet*) as it occurs in specific modes of fundamental attunements (*Grundstimmungen*). According to Heidegger these fundamental attunements are not subjective "feelings," as people would usually say, but rather overcome us and in such a way that they bring us before the bare fact of being and not-being as such. The fundamental attunement that Heidegger privileges in *Being and Time* is anxiety (*Angst*), but in other writings he focuses for instance on deep boredom (see the analysis of "tiefe Langeweile" in *Grundbegriffe der Metaphysik*)[11] or on wonder (the Greek *thaumazein*), or on reservedness or intimation (*Verhaltenheit* and *Erahnen* are fundamental attunements of which Heidegger writes in *Contributions to Philosophy*). By having us face the mere fact of being and not-being these fundamental attunements uncover a more fundamental sense or lack of sense in (not only our) being.

The thought of *Contributions* is the attempt at an original thought "of" be-ing in the sense that it is enowned by be-ing as event, that it is an answer to what gives itself to thought in our modern epoch. However, here thinking does not answer to something previously said. Rather this answering occurs in a specific attunement as be-ing gives itself to thought as an originating event. This is why Heidegger calls the thinking of *Contributions* inceptual (*anfänglich*). Together with be-ing this inceptual thought brings to language its own originating event. It thus requires an alertness to these inceptual moments of thought

where what we attempt to grasp and articulate is not yet quite clear and also reveals a dimension or aspects that escape our conceptual grasp. This alertness to
what remains ungraspable and/or calls to be brought to language is made possible and is guided by an attunement that reveals the withdrawing character of
what we try to say.

Similarly to the poet who thanks to an unusual openness to the world is
able to enclose in his words a more original sense of being, the thinking of *Contributions* attempts to move in a more original disclosure of being in its historicality. This disclosure occurs in a specific fundamental attunement that
Heidegger mostly calls "*Verhaltenheit*," "reservedness."

## b.   Thinking Be-ing in Reservedness

Resevedness, the fundamental attunement that, according to Heidegger, discloses
the event of be-ing for thought in our epoch is intrinsically complex. Heidegger
specifies two traits belonging to it: Startled dismay (*Erschrecken*) and awe
(*Scheu*).[12] In startled dismay, thinking is suddenly driven back (*fährt zurück*) by
the fact that in our modern epoch being has abandoned beings (*Seinsverlassen-
heit*), an abandonment that Heidegger thinks especially in terms of the historical
essence (Wesen) of technology that reduces things to mere means of production,
uprooting them from the "place" (earth and world) to which they originally
belong. He calls the mode of being that leads people to understand things only
calculatively as means of production "machination" (*Machenschaft*). In the reigning of machination be-ing discloses itself in its withdrawal (*Sichentziehen*) or refusal (*Verweigerung*).[13] But the dialogue with ancient Greek thought leads
Heidegger to think this self-concealment of be-ing not as a mere lack or negation
of being but as the way in which be-ing *is*, the way in which it occurs.

In Greek philosophy, being was thought as phusis, as letting-appear, as
bringing beings into presence. Beings that are thus brought into their presence
are *alethes*, true, or better *a-lethes*, not concealed. This leads Heidegger to think
the concealment as a more fundamental trait of be-ing. In its occurrence as
concealment being lets appear beings; be-ing in its temporality hides itself, so
to speak, behind the presence of things, and the coming-to-pass (the truth of
be-ing) that makes this presence possible remains unquestioned.[14] We find here
a historical explanation of what in *Being and Time* Heidegger calls Dasein's natural tendency to understand being analogously to the beings to which it relates:
Insofar as it brings to presence things, being itself guides us to think in such a
way that we first present to ourselves beings that we then take as a starting
point of whatever is not simply a being (whatever is thought to transcend

beings). This explanation is historical in a double sense: first, because it is thought in relation to ancient Greek thought as the cradle of Western culture and thinking; second because being itself is thought as an event: it is thought as a presencing withdrawal that in this withdrawal lets appear beings.

According to Heidegger the Greeks thought being only insofar as it lets appear things. Greek thought was born in wondering, the wondering of the *on he on*, of beings (not be-ing) insofar as they are. According to Heidegger, in our age we have little to wonder about: beings do not let us think any more the wonder of be-ing; thanks to technology they have become explainable, calculable, they have become means of consumption dragged into the whirlpool of technological evolution. This is why he would say that nowadays our original relation to the truth of be-ing discloses itself at first in startled dismay: the startled dismay of not-being.

In the startled dismay evoked by the abandonment of being, humans are set out (*ent-setzt*) from their usual relation with beings and are exposed to the strangeness (*Befremdlichkeit*) of be-ing.[15] But if humans are able to stand this state of be-ing, to remain attuned to it as they withstand the withdrawal, then in being-t/here (Da-sein) they hold open an original time-space of being in such a way that they allow be-ing to become manifest in its coming to pass. According to Heidegger the withstanding of the withdrawal of be-ing is made possible above all by a kind of awe (Scheu) that he also thinks as a gathering into a silence from which language may originally arise. Scheu usually means shyness, and the hesitation and delicacy of shyness are at play in such a way that they let be-ing *be*, they let be-ing occur in its truth, in its occurrence as disclosure-withdrawal. Thus, Heidegger says, awe brings close what is most remote.[16] In summary, the fundamental attunement of "reservedness" indicates a being set out from everydayness into the withdrawal of being that at the same time is withstood in awe in such a way that in this withstanding humans let be-ing occurs as such. This is where we should try to situate ourselves in order to appropriately question be-ing and through it beings (which includes, of course, bodies) as they occur in our time.

An analogy might be helpful in order to understand what Heidegger means when he writes that in startled dismay we are set out into the disclosure of the withdrawal of be-ing. It is not unlike what happens when suddenly an imminent death of a loved person is announced (or maybe our own death) and we are unsettled in such a way that we see the life of that person in the light of her passing. To attend to the dying person requires that we acknowledge and withstand in a kind of reservedness the fear of her passing. This loving attending would come close to the moment of Scheu (awe) to which Heidegger refers.[17]

Reservedness, like any "*Grundstimmung*" is nothing we could make or provoke ourselves. Rather it is a fundamental attunement that takes us and reveals the world as well as ourselves to us in a particular, original way. Only through this fundamental attunement can the original word come to a thinker or to a poet. Only through it, Heidegger would say, is an original destiny revealed to humanity.[18] Finally, it is only in such an attunement that we can realize that be-ing is not opposed to us is such a way that it could become an object of thought, but that it becomes manifest precisely in our being as a revealing-concealing event that first determines the way we come to understand ourselves.

In the event of be-ing we emerge (not simply from but) with a world and with other beings (living and nonliving). As is the case in Merleau-Ponty, this emerging occurs in differencing articulations, articulations that for Heidegger, however, do not necessarily end in a chiasmic otherness of I and world or I and other things. Above all, we do not come to stand before a "Being." Let us see, then, how in attuned-attunement to be-ing Heidegger articulates the "relation" between human being and be-ing "in general," granted that to speak of a relation between the two (as if they were entities) is inappropriate.

Heidegger characterizes the truth of being that is disclosed in reservedness as the oscillating movement between the throw (*Zuwurf*) of be-ing and the projection (*Entwurf*) or "counter-throw" (*Gegenwurf*) of *Da-sein*, or, in other words, between the call (*Zuruf*) of be-ing and correspondence (*Entsprechung*) of Da-sein.[19]

We may avoid misunderstandings by always translating Da-sein with being-t/here, since in *Contributions* Da-sein does not simply mean the being of humans. The "Da-" of Da-sein indicates the opening to the truth of be-ing, whereas the "-sein" indicates what Heidegger calls "*Inständigkeit*" ("insistence"), in contrast of the ek-sistence of which he speaks in the context of the earlier fundamental ontology. Insistence (or inabiding, as Emad and Maly translate) names the abiding in the opening of the truth of being as concealment-unconcealment. Taking up the previous analogy one may say that to abide in this opening is like attending the dying loved one instead of avoiding this difficult task by keeping oneself busy with other things. Heidegger thinks that by abiding in the withdrawal (the passing away) of be-ing humans find their originary being and the world, things, gestures, appear in a more essential dimension.

Being-t/here names the opening that is cleared in the middle of the truth of be-ing, into which in our times humans are set out in startled dismay and awe. It is an abysmal opening that exposes us to the passing away of be-ing. Thus the oscillating movement between being and being-/there is not simply one between Being and humans. Rather it is a movement in-between be-ing (that is experienced as passing away) and be-ing-t/here (the opening of and exposure to this passing), and it occurs in such a way that the "two" are opened *simultaneously*. Nothing is there prior to being-t/here that could be first thrown by a Being and then projected by being-t/here. There is no "entity" called Being that throws something to another "entity" called Da-sein insofar as be-ing is nothing but the event of a throw or thrust, a sudden opening in which being-t/here is enowned (*ereignet*). Being-t/here, in turn, is nothing but the disclosure of be-ing in its withdrawal. Being-t/here implies a "letting-be" of the withdrawing event of be-ing by yielding a historical time-space, a site in which it "appears." In German, the prefix "ent-" has the sense of "letting free," of "solving." Therefore the pro-jection (Ent-wurf) of being-t/here has the sense of a giving free, a bringing into the open the throw (Zu-wurf) of being. This, of course, requires humans as the ones who withstand the withdrawal of be-ing that consequently is not "made" by humans. Further this withstanding requires not only humans. There would be no being-t/here, no withstanding of be-ing's withdrawal, no abiding in its disclosure, without beings. A t/here of the event of be-ing is possible only if a being "shelters" this opening. Such a being may be a word, a work of art, a deed, a body. And as we will see, the sheltering into the body is at play not only as a specific mode of sheltering among others, but is intrinsically part of any mode of sheltering.

"Sheltering" expresses the particular way in which, according to Heidegger, things gather, delimit, and keep open a world and with it an originary sense of be-ing. In this word resonates the sense of a "keeping" that protects and lets be what it keeps. In it also resonates a sense of seclusion that points to the way in which things carry a sense of be-ing that always remains somewhat secluded and impenetrable, oscillating between disclosure and obfuscation. Thus the word "sheltering" refers us back to the attunement of reservedness that opens a sense of being in be-ing's occurrence as an opening and withdrawing, said briefly: in its truth.

c.   Sheltering the Truth of Be-ing in Beings

Before venturing further into what Heidegger calls the "sheltering of the truth of be-ing into beings" I would like to note that in the following account I will bracket the eschatological implications of Heidegger's thought. I will consider only marginally the historical frame of *Contributions* that situates thought in the experience of the possibility of an end of history in the total domination of *Machenschaft* and that sustains that our only hope is to help prepare the possibility of an other beginning of history. (It is here, it seems to me, that the worry of an impotency of humans toward their destiny makes very much sense.) This means that I will focus more on the "transitional" character of *Contributions* and on what happens in the words and thought of this book.

The possibility of such a reading is given by the fact that what Heidegger calls "*Bergung*," sheltering of the truth of being into beings, or the "grounding back" (*Rückgründung*) of beings into the truth of (their) being, can be seen in two different contexts: (1) With reference to the other beginning (that is the other beginning of Western history with reference to its first beginning in ancient Greece), it indicates the moment when maybe—in times to come—the originary coming to pass of be-ing as enownment manifests itself in the history of a people, where it pervades a particular world and a particular earth, opening new possibilities of being. (2) With reference to the transitional (*übergänglich*) thinking of *Contributions* (where a possible other beginning is prepared), one should also say that a sheltering occurs—if Heidegger's words are able to articulate the event of be-ing, however tentatively. A word is only able to say be-ing if it "shelters" this event, if in the words this event resonates not abstractly but in such a way that it resonates with our bodily being.

At this point we should consider also the difference between *bergen* and *verbergen*,[20]—that is, between sheltering and concealing. According to Heidegger, in metaphysics beings conceal the event of be-ing insofar as presented beings are the starting point for thought and insofar as the coming to presence and withdrawing that makes this presence of beings possible remains unquestioned. In the "sheltering" of the truth of be-ing this coming to presence and, most importantly for Heidegger, the withdrawing of be-ing finds an opening, a site. Since for Heidegger nowadays be-ing occurs as a refusal, as a gaping void behind the noise and increasing activity of machination, words (or works of art) shelter the truth of be-ing when they echo be-ing's withdrawal; that is, when they make manifest this void.

In order that a being may shelter the event of be-ing, humans must be set out into its abysmal opening and must withstand be-ing's withdrawal by abiding in this opening. Thus, in being (-sein) the "t/here," humans allow beings to shelter this opening. With the thought of sheltering Heidegger attempts to think beings from *within* an opening of be-ing in being-t/here. For Heidegger there remains a difference between beings and be-ing, a difference that is not the difference of two entities but of two intertwined events that occur within one another. As difficult as this thought of the "relation" between being and beings might be, it is clear that we cannot think one without the other. No truth occurs if not through beings that provide a site (time-space) for it. One may say that beings become transparent in their "thingness" in order to let shine through the event they shelter. We could not have any sense of the refusal of be-ing in the domination of machination if there were not a word able to say it and expose us to it, if there were not a painting that made it manifest. This is why in *Contributions* Heidegger speaks about a "simultaneity" (in quotation marks) of being and beings. It therefore appears curious that, besides emphasizing this "simultaneity," in *Contributions* Heidegger dedicates only a few pages to the issue of sheltering. But he does refer to his essay "On the Origin of the Work of Art,"[21] where he in fact thematizes this sheltering (Bergung). Thus "On the Origin of the Work of Art," an essay that Heidegger has reworked several times and that he wrote at the same time as *Contributions*, must be considered as an essential supplement to *Contributions*.

Since Heidegger's thinking is dedicated to the preparation of the "other beginning" of Western history, he attempts to think especially original modes of sheltering the truth of be-ing in beings as they occur in poetry, thinking, art, and in great political decisions.[22] In these original modes of sheltering, beings (words, works of art, political decisions) let shine through what Heidegger calls "*Urstreit*," the primordial strife between being and not-being—that is, between concealment and unconcealment. However Heidegger maintains that in order to be sheltered in a true entity, the original strife of truth must be transformed into the strife between world and earth.[23]

In "On the Origin of the Work of Art" Heidegger designates the world as the "reigning of vastness" (*waltende Weite*) where connections and paths open and where historical decisions of humanity take shape (Heidegger mentions birth and death, disaster and blessing, victory and disgrace, endurance and decline).[24] The earth, he says, is that on which humans found their living; it is that into which the arising "shelters back" (*birgt zurück*) everything that arises (humans, animals, plants, things).[25] Thus earth has the sense of an aspect of nature (nature not conceived as in natural science but more in the Greek sense of phusis); it comprises the passing away of natural things as well as their concealedness or hiddenness, which recalls the well-known fragment by Heraclitus: "Nature loves to hide" (*phusis kryptesin phulesthai*). The earth also has another, more narrow sense: It is that into which the work of art, words, and so on, set themselves back (*zurückstellt*). The work sets itself back "into the massiveness and heaviness of stone, into the firmness and pliancy of wood, into the hardness and luster of metal, in the brightening and darkening of color, into the clang of tone, and into the naming power of the word."[26] Here Heidegger thinks things (stone, wood, . . .) with respect to the way in which they are originally disclosed in being-t/here. They become manifest through their "qualities," their texture, through the way they *are*. This recalls to some extent the originary encounter with natural things of which Merleau-Ponty speaks in *The Visible and the Invisible*, although Heidegger would never speak of perception when describing this encounter. Natural things display a depth and "invisible dimension" that cannot be grasped objectively. The earth cannot be explained, it refuses itself to measurement and the calculability of science: the firmness and heaviness of the stone that are revealed in being-t/here, in an alertness to the originary emerging of be-ing, cannot be found by breaking apart the stone, by penetrating into it, or by weighing it.[27]

According to Heidegger world and earth are in an essential relationship where despite their radical difference they cannot be without each other. Whereas the earth always tends to seclude itself ("*Die Erde ist das wesenhaft Sichverschließende*")[28] and by secluding itself penetrates a world, the world always tends to open itself by grounding itself into the earth. "World and earth are essentially different from one another and yet never separated," Heidegger says.[29] They are in a strife insofar as the world cannot endure anything closed and that the earth tends always to draw the world into itself.

At this point one is tempted to identify the self-concealment of the earth and the opening of the world with the clearing of the truth of be-ing. But this would be inaccurate. The strife between world and earth always occurs with a specific world and a specific earth when they are held open in a particular work in being-t/here. With respect to the primordial strife of be-ing and not be-ing (as which the truth of be-ing occurs) the strife of word and earth appears to have a more delimiting determination that is tied more closely to the things that shelter this strife. Further, the originating motion does not start with things but with the clearing of be-ing. Thus Heidegger proposes a more accurate articulation of the occurrence of sheltering that would be said more "from" enownment: the truth of be-ing places and establishes itself (*richtet sich ein*) in the specific opening of a world and an earth by taking its stability from an entity that occupies this opening.[30] Because of its specificity this opening cannot exhaust the truth of be-ing that folds back on itself and withdraws as an abyssal and inexhaustible ground.

One could describe this event in terms of a differencing of the coming to pass of be-ing and the presencing of beings that is initiated in the withdrawing disclosure of be-ing. This means that the differencing does not lead to a seprartion of two distinct events or entities but rather to the concealment of the coming to pass (of the essential occurrence of be-ing that Heidegger also calls the strife between be-ing and nothingsness) that brings to presence beings and that finds a site only in this concealing presencing.

We therefore need to think a double concealment in the happening of the truth of be-ing: (1) the original self-concealment of the truth of be-ing in the strife of be-ing and nothingness that is tied to our experience of death and (2) the self-concealment of the truth of be-ing insofar as it is manifest in a particular being. By delimiting the original truth in a particular time-space, beings can conceal it (see metaphysical thinking where the original concealment of truth remains in its turn concealed insofar as be-ing is thought as presence) or make it appear as something that it is not.[31] We will see in what follows how this double concealment also occurs with and through human bodies.

## II. BEING AND BODY

### a.   The Role of the Body in the Sheltering of the Truth of Be-ing

So far Heidegger does not seem to have said anything explicit about the human body. However it is obvious that in the sheltering of the truth of being also the bodies of humans must play an essential role. In our common understanding we may consider human bodies not only as entities but also as belonging to and determining our being and comportments. Accordingly with respect to the sheltering of the truth of be-ing in beings we may consider the body as a being (work) that shelters/conceals truth, and also as a dimension of *being* t/here that allows for the sheltering of truth to occur in an entity.

Heidegger distinguishes two fundamental modes of sheltering in relation to the role we as humans play in it: creating and preserving (*Schaffen und Bewahren*). Creating concerns activities of production like, for instance, painting, building, or writing. Preserving concerns modes of being in which we attend to what is already there; for instance listening is a major form of preservation. It is obvious that we could do none of this without a body. How should we describe, then, the role of the body in sheltering? How should we speak of the body?

When attempting to answer these questions we should be careful not to jump ahead too quickly with familiar classifications. Along the lines of Heidegger's thought, we are looking for an originary determination of the human body, one that emerges in an experience of being-/there together with a sense of be-ing's withdrawal or passing character. Already in Merleau-Ponty's *The Invisible and the Invisible* it became clear that at the negative opening of being there is not yet a differentiation between perceiving and perceived between my body and other things. The original relation to our corporeality, much like that to bodies of other beings, is not yet differentiated into an interior and an exterior perception. Also, as the phenomenological analysis of Max Scheler suggest, we do not at first perceive a body (Körper) in another person and then deduce that it encloses a soul similar to ours, but we perceive "united totalities" (*einheitliche Ganzheiten*) that are not yet differentiated into interior or exterior perception.[32] Said in Heideggerian terms, we perceive the body as belonging to being-t/here; that is, it is originally disclosed in being-t/here and thus we need to think it from there. This means implicitly that we should let ourselves be guided by the attunements that open us to an original experience of being.

We may therefore try again to resist to our "natural" or "traditional" tendency to think the body with reference to its appearance as a thing. This is done by putting ourselves in the state of mind called *reservedness* that according to Heidegger opens the experience of be-ing peculiar to our epoch. As said before, reservedness implies that we are set out from our daily affairs with things into the experience of be-ing in its passing away or withdrawal and that we withstand this withdrawal. This withstanding keeps be-ing's withdrawal in a kind of hesitation (*Zögerung*), so that Heidegger speaks of a hesitating withdrawal of the truth (self-secluding opening) of be-ing. In this exposure to the hesitating withdrawal of be-ing a historical time-space of be-ing discloses. This time-space, that is the t/here of being-t/here, can persist only if it is sheltered in a being, which occurs through the creation or preservation of the opening.

Creation and preserving are the two modes in which humans abide in being-t/here, Heidegger even says that humans in their most originary possibility of being *are* the t/here. We may now add that humans abide in the t/here bodily (*leibhaftig*).[33] For how can a human abide in being-t/here if it is not in the first place his or her body that is exposed to be-ing's passing away and keeps this event open in specific ways? Is it not the body that delimits and opens a particular time-space, a concrete here and now in its taking place in difference *to* the withdrawing aspect of be-ing?

Like any being the body belongs to an earth and to a world. To its earthly quality would belong its specific texture, its mass, colors, movements, gender, and the sounds of our voices, and these would become apparent only in a world and its history, a history that, as time passes, inscribes itself into the lines of our face and into the aging skin, a history that in the fresh cheeks of a child is full of promises and open possibilities. In the context of how a world grounds itself into the earth we may also think of ways in which cultural practices and wars leave un-erasable traces in our bodies, traces that sometimes become visible in the movements of our bodies, in resistances and recurrent hesitations. In a body resonates a world and history that are not only of that body. The earth becomes apparent also in terms of the landscape and weather and also of the food that shape our body in its vitality (or lack thereof) and movements, all of which is discovered not in a static body-object but in the life of the body and its movements.

Like any being, the body may keep open or conceal being-t/here to different degrees. It may express (let shine forth, as Heidegger would probably prefer to say) the strife of earth and world or conceal it in its dull mass, which of course depends also on the sensibility (Heidegger would prefer to say abiding in being-t/here) of the one who sees and listens. Dancing would be an art in which the body could express most prominently this strife between an opening world and a secluding earth. But why should we not conceive that a simple gesture in an unexpected moment may do the same; it may express a moment of the history of a life (world) in its strife against finitude (earth), like an old man who sets down his walking stick with utmost care and hesitation before taking a step down the stairs, or a child who struggles to get a square block into its appropriate hole. Sometimes we witness such moments that despite their fleeting quality let resonate through silent gestures the mere fact of our and the other's existence in its passing quality, they open the moment of a whole life in its essential ungraspability.

In "The Origin of the Work of Art" Heidegger suggests that works (beings) cannot provide this site of be-ing directly but only through the strife or earth and world. However I think that the relation of the body to the truth of be-ing should not only be seen in relation to the opening and closure of a world and an earth. In its mortality the human body is not only related to a determinate world and earth but also to not-being as such, to the original self-concealment of the truth of be-ing. In section 202 of *Contributions* Heidegger says that the original concealment of be-ing is mirrored in death. Thus we distinguish ourselves in our corporeality at least from other nonliving beings[34] through our corporeal openness to the possibility of not being at all, and this being-towards-death, that according to Heidegger distinguishes us from all other beings, allows us to experience the withdrawal of be-ing as such. Said more simply, in facing our own mortality we experience the passing away that intrinsically belongs to all being.

Insofar as it provides a site for the disclosure of be-ing in its withdrawal the body is a threshold between being and not-being. Insofar as it is both a being and openness to be-ing the body is as well a threshold between be-ing and beings. As such it also is subject to the concealing that is proper to beings and that determines metaphysical modes of thinking. I may recall again the double concealment that according to Heidegger belongs to truth and that he elaborates already in his essay "On the Essence of Truth." In this essay he calls the more original mode of concealment "mystery" (*Geheimnis*) and the secondary mode of concealment "errancy" (*Irre*). Errancy is due to the fact that each being in its presence conceals the original concealment (the passing away) that belongs to be-ing. It is important to keep in mind that both modes of concealment always occur together. Thus the body both keeps open (in its mortality) and conceals (as a being) the passing-away that essentially belongs to be-ing.

## b.    The Corporeal Dimension of Being-T/here

What I here call body (Leib) is certainly a much larger "phenomenon" than what we usually call human body. It is not simply a conglomerate of organs and bones wrapped in muscles and covered by skin. Above all it is not limited by a subjectivity because in its mortality it is originally exposed to (and thus also shaped by) the coming to pass of be-ing and thus to other possibilities of being and to other beings.

The horizon of the body goes far beyond what we are used to see as the limit of our body. In "Building, Dwelling, Thinking" Heidegger says:

> When I go toward the door of the lecture hall, I am already there, and I could not go to it at all if I were not such that I am there. I am never here only, as this encapsulated body; rather I am there, that is, I already pervade the space of the room, and only thus can I go through it.[35]

I pervade the space not just with a projection of my mind in distinction to my body. Rather, I am bodily "ek-sistent" in space. This corporeal ek-sistence manifests itself also beyond the place that in a certain moment is reached by what we call our exterior senses. Let us take the famous example Heidegger gives of the bridge in Heidelberg:

> If all of us now think [. . .] of the old bridge in Heidelberg, this thinking toward that locale is not a mere experience [Erlebnis] inside the persons present here; rather, it belongs to the essence [Wesen] of our thinking *of* that bridge that *in itself* that thinking *persists through* [*durchsteht*] the distance to that locale.[36]

Here as well we need to think a corporeal ek-sistence that delimits and holds open the horizon of our thinking, even if it is certainly different from the "perception" of what can be reached through our "external senses." When we think about something or somebody far away in space or time (conceived in a traditional way) this implicates always a particular corporeal closure and opening to the world that occurs in certain states of mind (happiness or sadness, fright or calmness, etc.) more or less acknowledged.

The body of human beings (understood as corporeal ek-sistence) delimits the disclosure of a particular world. Yet there is always "something" exceeding the body as a given historical site (time-space) where a particular opening of the world occurs.[37] Viewed from within an originary experience of be-ing in its coming to pass, on the one hand this "excess" lies in the withdrawal that belongs to be-ing and that is a reserve of possibilities that may never find a site. On the other hand, an excess also occurs in the enowning (*Ereignung*), the thrust of be-ing that occurs as an opening of world and earth beyond what resonates in a particular being, as well as an opening of the dimension of the godly. All this can never be appropriated by one being or encapsulated in one body.

According to Heidegger be-ing occurs as enowning only when it is not distorted or covered over by machinationally disclosed beings. In the latter case Heidegger would say that beings remain dis-owned (*enteignet*) of their being. In our epoch, he would say, enowning is only possible in single and rare occasions. It marks that aspect of be-ing in which what comes to be is experienced in a sending (*Schickung*) or thrust (*Wurf*) to which thinking finds itself responding if it abides in being-t/here, in this exceptional opening where be-ing in its coming to pass is experienced as such. It is in such moments that we may recognize that the body in its delimiting ek-sistence is enowned. This does not mean that there is a Being that gives us our body. Enownment marks one moment in the experience of the disclosure of be-ing. The other (coconstitutive) moment is the response or counterthrow that first lets the enowning occur as enowning. Thus our corporeal existence expands in the counterthrow (*Gegenwurf*)[38] of be-ing's enowning throw (*ereignender Zuwurf*), it expands in its belonging to an earth and a world that at the same time it makes manifest as such. Consequently it is not appropriate to speak of the world as a "horizon" of the body, because this somehow implies that the body is subjective, that it "makes" its world. Rather we could say that the body takes place by differentiating itself from and within the opening of a world.

As noted earlier, the body differentiates itself from other beings through its possible opening to the original occurrence of truth. Precisely in this corporeal openness does the word come to the poet or the thinker, and does the artist create. It is here that we can be struck by the truth of a word in a work or in an action or that we may find ourselves in a strange intense proximity to another living being (an animal, for instance). From here we can also understand our openness to the other Da-*sein*. Even if we cannot transfer ourselves, so to speak, into another person, we can understand her (of course, within certain limitations) and let her be in her singularity and difference through our openness to the not-being that always encloses other possibilities of being. This would be the place from where one would have to approach the question of sexual difference in the horizon of Heidegger's thought in *Contributions*.

What happens in creative moments of corporeal openness directs the hand in writing, in painting or in making music; it directs the mouth in speaking, the human body in its gesture and in dancing. These actions remain without a "why," but they are certainly not without an origin in the sense of singular originating events that remain abysmal, inexplicable.

I have been speaking, up to now, more specifically about the human body understood as a corporeal ek-sistence in which it is open to its own finitude, to the finitude of other beings, and to the finitude of be-ing itself. In fact, only if in our being we acknowledge and withstand the passing away of be-ing that is mirrored in our own death does being-t/here authentically disclose. Only then do we experience the coming to be who we are in this event of be-ing, and we come to be who we are in our corporeal being. This brings along a couple of implications: Conceived in this openness to be-ing and as being enowned through be-ing, the body cannot be clearly delimited anymore to a human being. In its originary finitude our bodily being is open and exposed in being-t/here to the bodily being of other beings. Being-t/here itself (the in-between of the truth of be-ing) discloses "bodily" as a corporeal time-space, opened and delimited through different beings.[39] Said differently, being-t/here may be understood as the manifold of delimitations and openings of relations, junctures, differences in the world in which things "take place." Being-t/here and things take place in one occurrence.

The human body, my body for instance, is disclosed for me out of and within the corporeality of being-t/here; that is, out of delimitations and openings of beings that are disclosed with my own being. In a certain sense (even if it is only in the moment of not-being) my body *is* the body of beings that are disclosed with my own being. I am bodily open and exposed to other beings that are disclosed in my bodily being not only insofar as I understand them or relate "positively" to them, but even more in the manifold ways in which they remain hidden to my understanding or my awareness.

Of course there are innumerable ways in which in my being other bodies are disclosed for me. There are innumerable ways in which I find delimitations between what comes to appear to me as my body in distinction to (but not separate from) other bodies. There are different degrees of openness to beings as well as different degrees of awareness in this openness. And I would argue that the more one is open to and aware (in being-t/here) of the corporeal being of beings, the more one experiences their strangeness and difference, and the more one is likely to be changed or transformed in one's bodily being by other beings. But one should not forget also those silent transformations of bodies through practices and events that occur over generations, transformations that, when they occur, mostly escape our awareness.

## c. Bodily Thinking with and beyond Heidegger

With the consideration of the bodily dimension of being-t/here beyond the limits of a particular body and yet in conjunction with the being of a particular body we have brought Heidegger's thought very close to Merleau-Ponty's notion of flesh in *The Visible and the Invisible*.[40] In both cases the originary opening of the bodily dimension of being occurs through the finitude of being (in Heidegger articulated as withdrawal, in Merleau-Ponty as zero of being or nothingness). In both cases bodily being is thought as an opening, articulating event, although in different ways. A significant difference is found in the fact that Merleau-Ponty arrives at the bodily dimension of being through an analysis of perception, whereas in Heidegger we arrive at it through the disclosive power of an attunement to the withdrawing aspect of being. Further Merleau-Ponty's focus always remains the plenitude of being/s, and the negativity of being is thought only as passage, as an invisible that belongs to the visible, whereas in Heidegger the withdrawal or abysmal opening of be-ing functions like an origin out of which a world and earth disclose. We should note, however, that against the supposition of a negative ontology in Heidegger's work speaks Heidegger's thought that the originary ground (*Urgrund*) for Heidegger is not the abyss (*Abgrund*) but be-ing's occurrence as enowning; passing away is intrinsically tied to coming to be.

Another major difference between Merleau-Ponty and Heidegger is that Heidegger's thought in *Contributions* is framed by what the philosopher experiences as a historical necessity: the grounding of another beginning of history through the preparation of the grounding of being-t/here. There is no such project of a grand history of be-ing in Merleau-Ponty and I have pointed out above that in my exploration of the bodily dimension of being-t/here in Heidegger I have distances myself from this grand historical aspect of Heidegger's thought as well.[41]

The purpose of the present studies is the exploration of the bodily dimension in thinking. Along the lines of Heidegger's thought in *Contributions* we would have to say that this dimension discloses in specific attunements that set us out from everyday modes of being and into a situation where we experience be-ing as such. Here be-ing is experienced as an event of withdrawal or passing away but in this withdrawal also of a coming to be, of a disclosure of a world and earth as they become manifest through beings. For Heidegger essential thought occurs in attuned modes of *being*-t/here where thinking brings to language what gives itself to thought. This requires an alertness to attuned modes of being and the way in which they shape thought. Only through our corporeal opening in being-t/here are we able to think and say what we find in this opening. But at the same time this thinking and saying first makes manifest this bodily dimension of being. Heidegger calls this a "turning relation" (*kehriger Bezug*): Thought responds to the event to be-ing that first appears in this response through the words that are able to say this event.[42]

In this chapter I have argued that being-t/here occurs bodily. I have differentiated between the human body and bodily being-t/here and argued that the human body is (finds its being) in being-t/here. Since being-t/here discloses not only my being but also the being of other beings this means that my body is open to the being of others and to a historical world and earth that cannot be limited to what I come to understand as my own being in difference to others.

Thought arises in the opening of a world and earth that exceed myself and out of which my thinking can find words thanks to a corporeal ek-stasis in being-t/here. Along the lines of a thinking "from enowning," instead of speaking of corporeal ek-sistence (standing out) I should rather say that my bodily being emerges out of a corporeal opening and coexistence with other beings and that this opening is rooted in an exposure to death, to a nothingness that permeates all being in its coming to pass. So ultimately it is because the human body is as threshold between be-ing and not be-ing, as well as both a being and bodily ek-sistent in a world, that it can function as a site of articulation of be-ing, not only in its (the body's) life but also in language.

For Heidegger the nothingness that thinking needs to acknowledge in order to find an opening to be-ing's occurrence as enowning withdrawal carries epochal signification. It announces the possibility of an end of history for human kind through the total domination of machination. This would mean that being-t/here could not take place anymore, that there would be no more possible exposure to an essential dimension of be-ing and with it to others and to an earth and world in their strife.

In fact Heidegger suggests that viewed in terms of the lives of a people as a whole there is no time and place for essential modes of being-t/here. The very possibility of such a time-space first needs to be prepared and reawakened, a task that *Contributions* attempt to take up. For Heidegger, then, our bodies do not function as sites of exposure but of closure and forgetfulness. This closure is reinforced by the drive to always new excitements (*Erlebnis*) that we can see operate, for instance, in mass media production and consumption, but not only there.[43]

Heidegger certainly gives us insight into the dangers of our technological world, dangers we can hardly overestimate. But along with these dangers comes the danger that we focus only on the appearance of the global spectacle, projected by the workings of machination, and that we lose sight for the small singular events where something different happens. My strategy in facing the dangers of machination is rather to focus on these small happenings than on the big schemes, and I believe that Heidegger's focus on the grand history of be-ing made him blind to many other events.[44] I should add that at the same time the project of a history of be-ing has opened and sustained quite powerful thoughts and that my focus on small happenings may also be said to have its blind spot precisely when it comes to the bigger picture.

To release the historical frame (the transition from the first to the other beginning of Western history) within which Heidegger thinks the withdrawing event of be-ing certainly has an effect on how we experience and think the con-cealment/disclosure of be-ing and with it being-t/here. Now truth is only thought within the limit of a particular historical concealment/disclosure of beings in being-t/here and thus becomes essentially manifold. Truth, the con-cealment/disclosure of the coming to pass of be-ing is not held anymore in a tension that suggests a linear transition from *the* first to *the* other beginning of Western history. Instead it is just a disclosive as well as withdrawing bodily event in which we find innumerable openings, closures, junctures, differences, and lin-eages that are delimited and opened in our bodily ek-sistent being with other beings. Thus, bodies do not shelter *a* history of being but histories, crossing lin-eages that at the same time shape bodies in their movements and articulations.

With these considerations we open Heidegger's thought to Foucault's genealogical accounts of bodies, which are the subject of the next chapter.

*Chapter Six*

# Exorbitant Gazes
## On Foucault's Genealogies of Bodies

oucault's work is quite different from the writings of the philosophers that the previous chapters focus on, so much so that many
academics are not quite sure whether Foucault should be considered
a philosopher at all. Some people would rather call him a historian
or a structuralist, since his thinking neither moves in the paths of self-reflection
that characterize traditional philosophical thought, nor is it ontological in a
Merleau-Pontinian or Heideggerian sense. Foucault presents us with singular
descriptions of institutions, practices, and forms of knowledge and he traces lineages and shifts in constellations of power and knowledge that lead to new practices, different forms of knowledge, and ways of understanding subjects.

Foucault is not interested in finding first principles, in making universal
claims, or in thinking Being as such, and yet his thinking is interesting to scholars in philosophy precisely because he challenges traditional philosophical investigations. What makes him interesting for the present book is that he provides
us with a view of the bodily dimension in thinking that does not center in or
move along a direct experience of this dimension. At the same time his accounts
affect this dimension and thus the way we experience and think it. Foucault has
a strong sense of how institutions, practices, modes of knowledge, relationships of
power, and conceptions of truth play specific roles in shaping and transforming
bodies. He thinks these transformations of bodies and also the ways these affect
thought not from within attuned modes of being that he would attempt to express in a poietic language, but obliquely, from a distance, through descriptions of
archeological fragments and testimonies, which include in the first place texts.
Thus he directs our attention to concrete events and phenomena that shape and

transform the bodily dimension in thought, and he does this in quite different ways from the philosophers we have been considering so far.

If one can raise legitimate doubt as to whether Foucault should be called a philosopher in the traditional sense, one can as well raise legitimate doubt as to whether he should be called a historian in the traditional sense. Foucault's "histor-ical" analyses move as little along the lines of common historical practices as they move along the lines of a history of be-ing. He does not view historical events as a necessary concatenation of cause and effects and does not concentrate on world-historical events. Instead he focuses on seemingly marginal occurrences, like med-ical knowledge and practices, the arising of mental institutions, practices of punishment, penal laws, sexual practices and norms, and he describes shifts of power-knowledge relations within them. Further, Foucault does not claim to have the uninvolved "objective" eye that would give an uncompromised or "disinterested" account of historical facts, since he is well aware that his own thought is influenced by the practices and modes of knowledge that he describes and analyzes, and that his own writings may effect a change in relationships of power-knowledge. As Charles Scott writes, "Foucault's genealogy is implicated in what it comes to know and is epistemically involved in what it exposes."[1] There is, then, at least a philo-sophical vein in Foucault's writings if we understand philosophy as a questioning of ways in which we perceive and understand ourselves and the world we live in, so that the very principles by which we think are questioned and transformed.

The latest Foucault characterizes his whole work as being driven by the question of the relationship between subjectivity and truth. In an interview of January 20, 1984, he says that the problem of knowledge/power that many readers believe to be his primary interests, "is not for me [Foucault] the funda-mental problem but an instrument allowing the analysis—in a way that seems to me [Foucault] the most exact—of the problems of relationships between subject and games of truth."[2] Foucault continues to be read as a thinker of lib-eration who seeks freedom from oppressions, despite his continuing efforts in various interviews to expel that view. We will see further on in this chapter that such an interpretation is inconsistent with his understanding of how power re-lations work. Foucault's thinking certainly has political implications, but it is not driven by a political agenda (liberation of the oppressed), since this would reinscribe his thought in a teleologically driven discourse, which is exactly what his genealogical accounts undermine.

## a.    Foucault as Thinker from the Outside

I have already designated Foucault's thought as being a thought from the outside, and a few more explanations are required in order to clarify what I mean by this. Usually one pairs up the distinction between inside and outside with the distinction between subjective and objective points of view. But this would be misleading. In his own way, Foucault's thought is neither organized by the everyday subject-object distinction, nor by the way in which this distinction works in modern philosophy. By characterizing Foucault's thought as a thought of the outside I mean to say that his thinking remains outside the gravitational draw of a consciousness that focuses around the "I think." His Nietzschean heritage leads Foucault to see subjects as concepts and forms of being that are produced, multiple, and changing.

We saw in chapter 3 how Nietzsche radically undermines the unity of the "I think" when he understands it as the production of a multiplicity of forces. Yet we also saw that Nietzsche remains to a certain extent in the gravitational draw of reflexive consciousness when he claims that all thinking occurs in representations that appear to us as objects for a thinking subject, and that consequently we never will be able to think the world underneath and behind these representations. In other words, according to Nietzsche, we cannot escape the limitations of consciousness and its unifying draw, since all thinking occurs through consciousness.

By exposing the limits of consciousness Nietzsche brings up the question whether we can do away at all with consciousness without ceasing to think or simply becoming positivists. It appears that if we cease to reflect on the way we perceive or understand bodies we are left with a naive or unquestioned perception of bodies and remain unaware of the occurrences that influence and constitute this perception. This would mean that Foucault, in renouncing to a self-reflective approach to bodies, would operate with naive, unquestioned ways of thinking bodies. However I have just pointed out that he traces genealogically the formation of ways in which we conceive of bodies, and since Foucault is not interested in presenting a unified account of historical developments, he decenters and holds in question the formation of these concepts. Thus Foucault's thinking does not occur in the gravitational draw of consciousness or of a teleological account of a history of Western thought, but he thinks in the draw, or rather draws of what he attempts to think: lineages and transformations of power-knowledge relations that lead to different ways in which we become subjects.

Foucault does not think from "the" outside as opposed to a still presupposed primary "inside." Rather insides are continuously formed and transformed. The exorbitant gazes, with which I characterize Foucault's thought in the title of this chapter, do not refer to a single orbit. In a cosmological analogy one may say that he is neither thinking from the perspective of an inhabitant of the earth who perceives everything relative to his subjective position, nor is he thinking everything relative to our sun. He is rather thinking relative to the many solar systems that compose the cosmos in which we find ourselves, without attempting to trace them back to a first beginning. There is no single gravity at the center of Foucault's thought, but there are single trajectories, constellations, repulsions, and dispersions he follows and delineates. In this chapter I follow Foucault in his trajectories by specifically looking at how bodies come into play in them. As with the previous philosophers discussed in this book, I will not only look at how Foucault thinks bodies but also at how bodies and their formations play in his thought. We will look more specifically at bodies as sites of power-knowledge relations and, after problematizing this approach to bodies, as sites of care of the self. The texts from which this chapter draws are later texts of Foucault, which include *Discipline and Punish*,[3] the *History of Sexuality*,[4] especially volumes 1 and 3.

## b.   Genealogy

Before exposing ways in which Foucault thinks bodies we should consider more closely his approach; that is, how his genealogy presents us with a way of thinking reflexively outside of the gravitational draw of self-consciousness. Foucault describes genealogy as "a form of history which can account for the constitution of knowledge, discourses, domains of objects, etc. without having to make reference to a subject which is either transcendental in relation to the field of events or runs in its empty sameness throughout the course of history."[5] The knowledge, discourses, and domains of objects that interest Foucault are the ones that inform also his own thought, and he reflects on them genealogically by looking at the histories that constitute them. Thus, Foucault's thought does not come to stand against a history he could view objectively, a view that would assume a subject that transcends the historical occurrences it examines. Rather his thought and self-understanding remain caught in their own genealogy. To acknowledge this as a positive condition of thinking without trying to "escape" this involvement of thought in what it tries to think is essential for Foucault. Any urge to "escape" the opaqueness, finitude, and limitations that are intrinsic to the historicality of thinking indicate the urge for metaphysical principles, an urge that Foucault does not seem to have. In one of his last writings, an essay titled "The Subject and Power," Foucault says that his objective during the last twenty years of his life "has been to create a history of the different modes by which, in our culture, human beings are made subjects."[6] For Foucault, the subject, rather than being the source of a genealogy, is its objective. To be more precise, the objective is not "the" subject, as if there were only one, but different ways of subjectification. So, rather than positing or assuming a transcendental subject as a necessary correlate to the ways we understand the world and ourselves, Foucault questions how subjects are formed.

Foucault's genealogical reflection reaches toward the subject but not from it. It originates in a multiplicity of historical occurrences. It begins with occurrences that appear quite foreign to a reflective I, like torture practices or confessional practices in the seventeenth century, and follows oblique trajectories, which, through ruptures and transformations and without apparent inherent necessity, lead to an understanding of ourselves as subjects today, as subjects who find themselves exposed to and informed by a multiplicity of events we could never appropriate, even as we attempt to do so. Genealogical reflection thus falls back unto that which informs it from the beginning, namely the experience that the ways we understand ourselves are informed by lineages well beyond our time and places or the skin that surrounds our physical bodies. And yet, what interests Foucault when he traces the genealogy of modes of subjectification is what is closest to us. In "Nietzsche, Genealogy, History" Foucault designates the genealogical approach to history as "effective history": "Effective history," he says, studies what is closest, but in an abrupt dispossession, so as to "seize it at a distance."[7] This "abrupt dispossession" indicates that the distance from which genealogy seeks to describe "what is closest" is not possessed by a subject, it is not in the orbit of subjectivity and does not provide a firm ground for it. We cannot find a hold for our self-understanding in genealogy because there is no firm basis to start from, no ultimate true fact, no true origin. In fact truth too is historical, and thus changes through different discourses, practices, and modes of knowledge in different societies.

One could think, then, that the genealogical trajectories Foucault chooses are totally random, and, indeed, there must be a randomness to them since he does not claim any necessary connection between certain occurrences in the past and occurrences in the present. There is no claim that the history he tells is *the* truth or reveals *the* truth about how we become subjects. But it is not mere invention either. For Foucault there are truths and these truths can function as such only if they have some hold in reality. He concludes an interview concerning *The History of Sexuality* by saying: "I am well aware that I have never written anything but fictions."[8] But he also adds: "I do not mean to say, however, that truth is therefore absent. It seems to me that the possibility exists for fiction to function in truth, for a fictional discourse to induce effects of truth, and for bringing about that a true discourse engenders or 'manufactures' something that does not as yet exist, that is, 'fictions' it. One 'fictions' history on the basis of a political reality that makes it true, one 'fictions' a politics not yet in existence on the basis of a historical truth."[9]

Genealogy, then, does not just look at past events as if they stood by themselves, but produces "truths," it effects among other things ways of understanding ourselves that have a truth claim in that we recognize ourselves in them.[10] This self-recognition could be overturned shortly after by another "fiction," and yet, this new fiction, like any one that is effective in the production of truth, cannot be totally random but must find at least some basis within a system of truths that functions in a specific society.

Genealogical reflection accounts for the ways subjects are constituted as it transforms the constitution of subjects. It should be clear that this transformation is not just an innocent by-product of Foucault's genealogy but that it is part of the objective of his genealogy. It is because Foucault seeks a transformation of how subjects are constituted that he never follows established mainstream explanations of historical events but looks at what appears marginal or accidental, and that he reverses patterns of explanations. This concerns especially his exploration of how power-knowledge relations effect lineages and their historical transformations. It is important to note that even if it is Foucault's objective to transform ways of subjectivation, he has no interest in prescribing how we should understand ourselves as subjects or what practices we should follow in order to become "better" people. The issue for him is to keep open possibilities of transformation and not to set down new rules.[11]

Foucault's exorbitant gazes do not look at a subiectum that is already there but they seize their objectives as they are constituted in their sights in the crossing of multiple historical trajectories. At the same time, they do not seize a mere fiction but subjects in which we recognize ourselves. But how are we to understand these subjects in whom we recognize ourselves? And how can we come to such a recognition if these subjects are not properly a subiectum, something underlying our recognition, but are rather the effects of the crossing of historical lineages and genealogical inquiry?

Like Nietzsche, Foucault understands subjects in relation to a multiplicity of forces and power-knowledge relations that are discovered by paying attention to the body. Therefore it might be helpful to recall how Nietzsche accounts for the constitution of subjects. In a fragment of 1885 he writes:

> The body and physiology the starting point: why?—We gain the correct idea of the nature of our subject-unity, namely as regents at the head of a communality (not as "souls" or "life forces"), also of the dependence of these regents upon the rules and of an order of rank and division of labor as the conditions that make possible the whole and its parts. In the same way, how living unities continually arise and die and how the "subject" is obeying and commanding, and that the struggle expresses itself in the limits of power is part of life.[12]

The subject, understood as a unity with which we identify ourselves, is like the summit of a hierarchical order. According to Nietzsche, we identify ourselves with a feeling of power within this hierarchical order: "The subject:

this is the term for our belief in a unity underlying all the different impulses of the highest feeling of reality."[13] In contrast to Foucault, when Nietzsche looks at the body and at the multiplicity of struggling forces he finds within it, he remains mostly within the motion of traditional reflexive thought; he remains in a mode of self-examination. He also remains within traditional subjective thought in that he runs against an epistemological problem: Thinking the body for him means to objectify it. But then, as object of thought, it becomes mere fiction, an object of consciousness, a unity that has lost the multiple constitutive forces operative underneath this objectification.

For Foucault this epistemological problem is no problem at all, since he does not take a subjective trajectory and he does not presuppose that there is something like one true determination of the body. He does not ask the "what" question; he does not ask what is the body?—a question that would suggest that he views the body as an object of thought—but rather he looks at different sciences and practices and at how in them the body functions as a site for power-knowledge relations.

The fact that Foucault sees bodies as sites of power-knowledge relations does not mean that he considers bodies to be subjugated to and molded by outside forces and powers. He describes power as "a way in which certain actions modify others"[14] and distinguishes it from violence in that power presupposes an amount of freedom on the side of the one on which it is exercised: "Faced with a relationship of power, a whole field of responses, reactions, results, may open up."[15] This means that as a site of power-knowledge relations the body is an open as well as a delimited site of constraints and resistances. Knowledge occurs both as a result of power and it informs power. For instance, supposed knowledge of behavioral patterns may induce power relations in order to form specific behaviors. Thus the knowledge that repetition of a certain vocabulary will result in the use of that vocabulary induces schools to adopt repetition as a practice. But knowledge also results from power relations when these make visible for instance behavioral patterns. For example one can form knowledge about human behavior by confining and observing prisoners.

To conceive the body as a site for power-knowledge relations leads to quite diverse ways of understanding bodies. In the following section I will briefly look at the various ways in which, especially in *Discipline and Punish* and *The History of Sexuality*, Foucault thinks of bodies.

## c.  Bodies as Sites of Power-Knowledge Relations

In *Discipline and Punish* and *The History of Sexuality* (vol. 1) Foucault thinks bodies in the manifold ways in which they are objectified through different

sciences as well as in the manifold ways they are targets of disciplinary practices. He thereby distinguishes especially specific practices of punishment and
confession in Europe before and after the eighteenth century. In practices up
to the eighteenth century, the body appears as target for the infliction of punishment or as a target for the extortion of truth. In descriptions of practices of
torture bodies appear in their fleshly qualities; one can inflict physical pain by
severing limbs or by burning or cutting skin.

With the eighteenth century becomes more prominent what Nietzsche
describes in *The Genealogy of Morals* as a movement of interiorization, where
punishment is less directed at torturing the flesh and more at "torturing" or in-
flicting restraints upon the "soul" through disciplinary practices. Foucault understands this "soul" not in opposition to the body but as a product of the
workings of power/knowledge in specific practices. The soul is not a substance
one could separate from the body. According to Foucault, it "is produced permanently around, on, within the body by the functioning of a power that is ex-
ercised on those punished."[16] A soul is produced, for instance in practices of
religious confession when the confessed feels guilt for having stepped over certain rules. A soul is also produced when a prisoner, after a long period of con-
finement, starts dissociating something like a free "inner" self from the
constrained body. Thus, the soul arises out of and within certain ways in which
the body is affected and "effected" by power-knowledge practices. From a practice of physical punishment by means of torture, severing of limbs, death, and
so on, punishment turns into disciplinary practices that aim at transforming the
ways in which bodies behave and feel by affecting and "effecting" their souls.

The body becomes more and more a target of disciplinary practices that
aim at the production of "docile bodies." This happens not only in prisons but
also in schools, military camps, factories, and other institutions. Bodies are
trained to function according to timetables, to divisions of spaces, and prescribed
orders of movement. Concurrently, the new human sciences arise, like medicine,
psychiatry, criminology, and demography, which each objectify bodies in different ways and thus produce different "truths" about bodies. The discoveries of
these sciences profit as much from the division of spaces, time tables, and other
disciplinary elements as these disciplinary practices profit from the "discoveries"
of the human sciences, which will allow for more refined practices.

Bodies are trained and objectified by virtue of power-knowledge relations. Foucault describes this quite effectively with Bentham's Panopticon,
where bodies are kept in single cells and are continuously exposed to the surveillance of gazes that one supposes to be in a central surveillance tower. For the
individual under surveillance the controlling gazes remain invisible and anony-
mous. This means that there may not even be any controlling gazes in the sur-

veillance tower; the tower may be left empty and the power structures would still work in the same way. The panopticon is a symbol and exemplar of a decentralized and desubjectivized model of the workings of power-knowledge relations. In modern society, there is no visible centralized power acting upon a body like in times where a regent had absolute power over the lives of his subjects. Rather power works within the individual's "docile bodies." What counts is that individuals feel themselves observed, that they bend to the invisible gaze of a supposed controlling agent, a controlling agent they have totally incorporated so that the same body is a site of control and submission.

Panopticism is a model of the workings of power-knowledge relations that effects a normalization of bodies not just on the surface but in depth and without the mediation of consciousness. Foucault writes that "power-relations can materially penetrate the body in depth, without depending even on the mediation of the subject's own representations. If power takes hold on the body, this is not through its having first to be interiorized in people's consciousness."[17] Foucault is not saying that we never are conscious of the ways in which our bodies automatically follow certain regulations, like showing up timely in school, stopping at a red light, feeling urged to confess an "error," walking on the sidewalk instead of on the street, reordering the silverware and plate on a table before starting to eat, expecting people to have heterosexual partners). The point is that it is not necessary for us to be conscious of these workings of power-knowledge relations: they work regardless. Our bodies are preconsciously exposed to power-knowledge relations that transverse and shape our bodies in their habits.

As noted above, Foucault's descriptions of power-knowledge relations use an "objective" language. He does not speak of his experience of them, he does not say how one feels in them (as if they took place within a subject) or reacts to them (as if they came from "outside" of a subject); he describes them as if they were independent from his accounts. But since Foucault's genealogy is aware that it uncovers modes of subjectivation (becoming subjects) that also effect and affect genealogical practice and new possibilities of subjectivation, it is not merely "objective." This becomes more apparent when we take into account the reader of his genealogy.

As readers of Foucault's genealogical accounts we find our bodies at once dispossessed and intimately affected; we find our bodies to occur as nonsubjective sites of power-knowledge relations. What happens is not that we project "our" bodies onto the workings of power/knowledge Foucault describes, but rather that we find our bodies affected out of these descriptions as they mirror seemingly strange events. We find our bodies in a dispossessed way as we for instance recognize processes of normalization, let's say of sexual normalization, which give priority to heterosexual relations between adult couples. We find our bodies out there in descriptions of torture practices in the seventeenth century or of prisons in the eighteenth century as we experience resistances to power and motions of power in which we find ourselves empowered. Many readers experience resistances to the "groundlessness" of Foucault's descriptions, to the lack of a teleological framework or to the feeling of exposure with regard to what they are used to understand as their intimate self. But the reader of Foucault's "dismantling" description of panopticism may also feel herself empowered by the fact that she has seen through this mechanism, as if this knowledge gave her a new freedom.

By pointing to the way Foucault's genealogy affects us I am moving to a way of speaking that draws from what we usually would call subjective experiences. Foucault clearly avoids such ways of speaking, which means that I am moving out of Foucault's frame of thought. But to describe the ways we are affected when we read Foucault cannot simply mean a return to subjective experiences conceived in a traditional way, since Foucault's genealogy deconstructs the subject understood as an underlying entity precisely at the experiential level. We experience the motions we find in our bodies not as our possessions. If anything, we are possessed by them as if they were most intimate strangers. So even if we do go beyond Foucault when we consider the effects of his texts on the reader, we do so in the echo of an estrangement that his descriptions continue to carry with them. One could also say that even if we move away from a Foucaultian approach to power-knowledge issues, we do so in attunement with his text.

Foucault dispossesses the subject that Nietzsche describes as a feeling of unity in a hierarchical order of drives and resistances, and as a feeling that derives from the fact that we identify ourselves with the strongest feeling of power at work in this hierarchy. Foucault's genealogical descriptions subvert hierarchies as they show us multiple divergent origins of forces and resistances that we find in our bodies, origins clearly outside of the grasp of a subject or unifying reasoning. There is no unity left with which we could identify ourselves, at least not a stable one that could claim some ultimate truth for herself. Our very bodies are multiple and dispersed since the ways we experience and understand them are dependent upon manifold practices and modes of knowledge that in turn manifest different forms of power-knowledge relations.

If we attempted to summarize the different determinations of bodies that we find in Foucault's *Discipline and Punish* and *The History of Sexuality* (vol. 1), we may come to the following classification (and we should keep in mind that Foucault does not ask the What? question but rather questions the way certain concepts and practices operate):

Bodies become sites of power-knowledge relations (1) as targets of practices and (2) as targets of knowledge:

1. Bodies as targets of practices appear (a) as visible flesh upon which one can inflict pain and from which one can extort truth through practices of torture; and (b) as docile bodies that are disciplined in various institutions: schools, military camps, prisons.

2. Bodies as targets of knowledge, especially of the human sciences, acquire different determinations according to the sciences that objectify them: medicine, psychiatry, criminology, demography.

We may add that these determinations carry with them different ways of understanding or rather of producing truths about the body and also different modes of subjectivation.

## d.   The Outside of Power-Knowledge Relations

In the classification of different ways of targeting and conceiving—and thus producing—bodies, which I just offered, I have followed Foucault in his predilection for structures and classifications. Foucault's practice of dividing and classifying different elements in his genealogical accounts reveals a discipline whose mechanisms he analyzes in his texts. These mechanisms characterize disciplinary practices that go along with the formation and development of the human sciences since the eighteenth century. Foucault exposes them, for instance, in the model of the panopticon: Single cells divide the subjects that thus can become objects of scientific experiments and observation that may lead to classify forms of behavior and other things. There certainly remains a significant difference between these sciences and Foucault's practice of systematization and classification: In Foucault these practices are not guided by a unifying principle or telos, or by a practical goal. In many cases his classifications appear to be useless; they seem to be fragments from a past that cannot be recuperated anymore.

The fact that Foucault's writing manifests power-knowledge relations whose lineages he describes in his texts, the fact that apparently any practice or form of knowledge is sustained by power relations leads to a sense of claustrophobia in many readers. If, together with Foucault, we abandon all transcendental principles, it appears that all that we are left with are shifting power-knowledge relations.

Can we, then, not strive beyond our human conditions? And is this striving, as Kant felt so vividly, not part of our human condition? With these questions we approach a threshold that marks contemporary European and Continental philosophy in its questioning and/or attempt at overcoming metaphysics. It is worthwhile, then, to dwell some more on the sense of claustrophobia and of a physical resistance that many readers of Foucault experience.

The reader that experiences an uneasiness or—maybe more intensely— a physical resistance to Foucault's descriptions of power-knowledge relations must admit that such resistance is possible only if one is intimately affected by Foucault's accounts. As noted above, in reading his text the readers' bodies become sites of power-knowledge relations, and this seems all the more to make a case for what Foucault claims.

From this site of resistance to Foucault's text one may go in two opposed (and thus also related) directions. On the one hand one may see such resistance as a symptom of embodied transcendental structures; the principles that have governed our thought are shaken and the site of the dead god, announced by Nietzsche, loses its hold. The Foucaultian claim would be that once we let go of it we enter a space of transformation that can allow for new possibilities of thought. On the other hand one may interpret this resistance as a "healthy" resistance to the danger of a closure of thought to new possibilities of thinking in an endless circling of power-knowledge relations. It would also be a resistance to the limited conception of a body that bends it's functioning to the workings of power mechanisms and the knowledge that produces them and is produced by them.

It is safe to say that Foucault would not be happy with such a scenario either. To "cut the regent's head off," to deconstruct subjectivity, to disrupt patterns of normalization, all these are not simply side-effects of Foucault's genealogy but they are concerns that inform his thought, that give it shape and direction. Like in other deconstructive thinkers, in Foucault's thought the subversion of established orders and hierarchies carries a political dimension. He looks for new ways of thought and for different ways of subjectification, and this means that he looks for a transformation of our bodies, conceived as sites of power-knowledge relations.

However if a text's meaning cannot be reduced to the supposed intentions of the author when he wrote it, if we also need to take into account its effects on the readers, then the danger of a closure of Foucault's texts in the circling of power-knowledge relations remains.

In fact Deleuze claims that Foucault himself felt uneasy about the possibility of remaining trapped within power-knowledge relations. Deleuze begins the last chapter of his book *Foucault* by saying: "What happened during the fairly long silence following *The History of Sexuality*? Perhaps Foucault felt slightly uneasy about the book: had he not trapped himself within the concept of power-relation?"[18] But he then argues that Foucault also thinks something that escapes the trap of established power relations, namely a life that Deleuze designates as the force of the outside. Deleuze suggests that according to Foucault "power does not take life as its objective without revealing or giving rise to a life that resists power; [. . .] the force of the outside continues to disrupt the diagrams and turn them upside down."[19] According to Deleuze, the force of the outside is "like a new axis, different form the axes of both knowledge and power."[20] He calls this third axis, which according to him is present in Foucault from the beginning, "self." The self, he explains, is the fold of the outside.[21] The fold of the outside creates always changing ways of subjectification. This means that the outside is not some kind of separate space acting upon an interiority. As fold of the outside the interiority of the subject (self) is coextensive with the outside. By speaking of a fold of the outside Deleuze attempts to articulate an other to power-knowledge relations that at the same time does not transcend them. This other is linked to the self, that is, to the issue that the late Foucault sees as a main question of his thought.

But Deleuze ultimately links the outside, together with power and knowledge, to thought. He says: "In truth, one thing haunts Foucault—thought. Knowledge, power, and self are the triple root of a problematization of thought."[22] This appears to draw Foucault's genealogy back into the realm of consciousness, but the reflexivity of this conscious thought has its source in an outside that Deleuze further describes as a "line that continues to link up random events in a mixture of chance and dependency."[23] Thought draws from the outside "particular features" that include "particular features of power, caught up in the relations between forces; features of resistance, which pave the way for change; and even savage features which remains suspended outside, without entering into relations or allowing themselves to be integrated."[24] Savage features are features that cannot be integrated into experience, so that part of that from which thought draws its features resists experience. It is probably the mixture between features of resistance and savage features that accounts for the disruptive force of the outside and allows for different ways of thinking.

If we try to see concretely in Foucault's text where these features from the outside are (something that Deleuze does not do) we may, for instance, find features of power in Foucault's descriptions of modes of punishment, and features of resistance in counterpractices of knowledge that transform these modes of punishment. As for savage features, these may be practices and forms of knowledge that Foucault describes and that simply disappear since they do not find space in new power-knowledge relations.

Deleuze does not say much of the body's role in this folding of the outside that is coextensive to the self and that he attributes specifically to thought. According to the exposition given earlier in this chapter, the bodily dimension in thinking that is specific to Foucault's text can be found in the way it exposes the reader to power-knowledge relations from a distance. When reading Foucault, we find our bodies out there in strange descriptions of power relations that at the same time may affect us intimately. We may experience multiple draws, ruptures, resistances that, as Deleuze suggests, can be conceived as folding from the outside such that they form our empirical subjectivities. We may say that our bodily "selves" are constituted by features of power, by features of resistance, and by savage, "disconnected" features, which, by the way, is not unlike the bodily dimension that appears in Nietzsche's text. Possibilities of transformation arise in this exposure to an outside that is in Foucault's text when we read it, but that, far beyond the effects of his text, extends to any power relations and forms of knowledge as well as to "savage features" that form and transform our subjectivities. Thinking along with Foucault is one means by which we may actively remain exposed to the outside of particular power-knowledge relations that have shaped our bodies over a period of time. But it is not clear to me that thinking is therefore "the one thing" that "haunts" Foucault, as Deleuze says. Such a statement underscores the importance of practice, for instance of practices of care of the self to which the latest Foucault gives most of his attention.

### e.   Bodies as Sites of Care of the Self

Maybe it is only when we follow Foucault into the last phase of his thinking that we can counter effectively the risk of remaining caught in an endless circling of power-knowledge relations to which we appear to be hopelessly exposed. Up to that point, Foucault's thinking is prominently deconstructive: In its genealogical accounts it undermines transcendental ways of thinking and it exposes the ways in which our bodies are shaped in power-knowledge relations that are beyond the grasp and control of a single subject. Even if this opens new possibilities of thinking and practice that allow for new forms of subjectivities to arise, Foucault's focus on coercive practice and forms of scientific knowledge did not make quite clear what could be appealing about this. From coercions between a regent and his subjects we move to "internalized" coercions and formations of docile bodies. The body becomes a target of medical and psychiatric knowledge that also appear as arbitrary forms of constraint in their claims to truth. At the same time Foucault makes clear that we cannot escape being caught in power-knowledge relations. Certainly, he always adds that this implies a certain amount of freedom, but it is curious that many readers continue to overlook this.

Perhaps it is only in Foucault's genealogy of the care of the self in the Greco-Roman world that the freedom inherent in power-knowledge relations becomes more apparent. Foucault suggests that in Greek and Roman civilizations practices of care of the self "had a much greater importance and auton-omy than later on."[25] That he sees in these practices of the self a prominent possibility of freedom not only for the people of that era also is suggested by what he says in the interview of January 20, 1984:

> I don't believe there can be a society without relations of power, if you un-derstand them as means by which individuals try to conduct, to deter-mine the behavior of others. The problem is not of trying to dissolve them in the utopia of a perfectly transparent communication, but to give one's self the rules of law, the techniques of management, and also the ethics, the *ethos*, the practice of self, which would allow these games of power to be played with a minimum of domination.[26]

Practices of care of the self are practices of self-formation that make manifest far more than Foucault's descriptions of coercive practices what he calls "practices of freedom." Such practices should be distinguished from a common understanding of liberation, as when prisoners are released or when a revolution frees a people from a despotic ruler. Such forms of liberation are no guarantee for the freedom of people that, Foucault says, can take place only in a continuous practice of freedom. Practices of freedom occur within power-knowledge relations.[27] We already saw above that for Foucault freedom is in-trinsic to power in that the exercise of power presupposes a possible resistance to power as well as the possible compliance of the one upon which power is ex-ercised. Practices of freedom also imply knowledge in that the knowledge of different possibilities of action and resistance, of different rules or principles of conduct one could adopt, is necessary in order not simply to perpetuate exist-ing power relations. The body, then, is not only a site of power/knowledge but also a site for the practice of freedom, for instance through the care of the self.

Like in his previous writings, Foucault's genealogical approach in the third volume of *The History of Sexuality* ("The Care of the Self") reveals dis-continuities, ruptures, diverse discourses occurring at the same time, but also some recurrent traits. The topic of the *cura sui* proposes again a version of Socrates' "Know Thyself!" and recommendations of certain restraints in sexual activities seem to announce Medieval moral codes. And yet Foucault also sees significant ruptures between the different epochs. He emphasizes that recom-mendations of sexual moderation and abstinence that one can find in stoic texts do not associate the sexual act with evil as in the Middle Ages. Further there is an emphasis on the individual who imposes rules on himself for the sake of a better life. Rules are not imposed from above but are the result of a number of concerns for the body and for the soul.

The self-imposition of rules of conduct that Foucault describes is as much a practice of freedom as Foucault's approach insofar as it does not suggest that some rules are better than others and insofar as he does not suggest necessary "evolutions" or causal chains from one stage of history to the next. Instead he leaves space for contingencies, exceptions, unforeseeable changes, and possible self-determination through individual judgments.

Along with a practice of freedom the care of the self highlights another aspect that earlier texts of Foucault emphasize less: The role of pleasure in the formation of the self. Pleasure takes different forms and has varying places in the cura sui. Foucault writes that according to Seneca pleasure is the result of a "self-possession" or "mastery over oneself": "The individual who has finally succeeded in gaining access to himself is, for himself, an object of pleasure."[28] In other texts philosophers recommend that pleasure should not be taken as a goal of a relationship but that it is a by-product of a well-formed relationship. In general, regimens of pleasure "are more 'concessive' than 'normative'," says Foucault.[29] The issues are that of the right age, the right time, and the right measure, and not one of prohibition. The idea that pleasure itself is bad would arise only later, in the Middle Ages.

An understanding of bodies as sites of practices of freedom and of pleasure (within power-knowledge relations) suggests different possibilities to find and create truth about oneself. Thus one is not simply an object of truth as it is conceived by various sciences, or a site of extortion of truths in confessional practices; there is also the possibility of creating truths about oneself in practices of care of the self. We should note that there is no indication by Foucault that "self-made" truths are better truths than ones that are suggested by a science. This is also the case because practices of care of the self remain exposed to institutionalized practices, customs of a people, and forms of knowledge in different sciences (medicine, psychology, astrology). Further, the care of self is not an egoistic or egocentric practice. As Foucault writes: "all this attention to the self did not depend solely on the existence of schools, lectures, and professionals of spiritual direction for its social base; it found a ready support in the whole bundle of customary relations of kinship, friendship, and obligation."[30]

Although it involves forms of knowledge and conceptions of truth, the issue of subjectivity that the latest Foucault approaches in a genealogy of the care of the self is in the first place an issue of praxis. Foucault's interest in modes of subjectivation is an interest in concrete practices that shape not just our understanding of who we are but our very "physical," lived selves. He thus emphasizes an aspect of philosophy that was there in the beginning of Western philosophy in the figure of Socrates, that had a revival in early Roman philosophers, and that then slowly moved into the background of philosophical disputes and writings: the "art of existence."

This emphasis on the care of oneself sheds a new light on the bodily dimension in thinking as we may find it through Foucault's texts. This bodily dimension not only is informed by multiple lineages, relations of power within society, and modes of knowledge, it also reaches back into lineages in formation, into relations of power and into different ways of forming, understanding, and encountering oneself and others. Thus, as a practice of uncovering and reconstructing these lineages, genealogy is not simply a theoretical philosophical activity but it belongs into an ethos of living.

## f.  Conclusion

Foucault's genealogy traces multiple connected and disconnected lineages that account for the formations of subjectivities that in these very genealogical accounts again appear as transforming sites of power-knowledge relations. One may suspect that Foucault's continuous concern for subjectivity appears to be yet another Cartesian heritage. However this concern arises precisely out of an understanding that there is no transcendental subject, no ultimate self, and that the truths we form around these historically determined inventions of a self shape and determine our *ethos*—the way we live. Thus, the bodily dimension in thinking clearly appears to be not centered in a thinking subject; rather it is dispersed histories of practices and modes of knowledge the effects of which Foucault makes manifest to us as we read his texts.

At the beginning of this chapter I pointed out that Foucault's way of thinking differs significantly from the other philosophers considered in the present book. The performativity of his thought is not present in such a way that we can move along it reflexively. In order to articulate the bodily dimension of his text I had to take into account its effect on the reader. This means that in order to trace the bodily dimension of Foucault's thought I had to translate his impersonal accounts into an experience of thought that I could access reflexively. Thus we cannot even say that the bodily dimension that thereby becomes apparent is properly Foucault's. This demarcates a limit both of the project of the present book and of Foucault's thought. The limit of the present project becomes apparent in that the issue of the bodily dimension in thinking clearly requires a reflexive approach that takes into account the way we experience thinking as we think. The limit of Foucault's thought becomes apparent in the fact that his texts do not present such an approach. Foucault does not trace the arising of his thought as he thinks. This allows him to stay away from a unifying subjectivity in his thought but it also entails a certain ambiguity of the concepts he uses. He just takes them as they appear in the texts he studies without attempting to mediate between different ways of "using" the same word or establishing some kind of fundamental meaning. Consequently also the concept of "body" remains quite unclear and ambiguous in his writings, even if one can try to enumerate different ways in which it is used or appears in different writings.

But even if there is a limit between a reflexive approach to the bodily dimension in thinking (and by reflexive I do not mean "within" a consciousness that understands itself as being distinct from a world) and Foucault's thought, this does not mean that there is untranslatability between the two approaches, as the present chapter attests. Here we need to abandon the idea that translation only means the transposition of an identical meaning from one language to another, or, in this case, from one approach to another. Such idea of translation is not only questionable but proves useless in this case. The issue is rather to let one approach "inform" the other, "inform" in the literal sense of "shaping in." In this sense Foucault "informs" the question of the bodily dimension in thinking in that it exposes limits and aspects of this dimension that otherwise could remain concealed.

# Concluding Prelude

Throughout the explorations of the bodily dimension in thinking in my readings of Plato, Nietzsche, Scheler, Merleau-Ponty, Heidegger, and Foucault, a recurrent theme is the desubjectivation of thought. To a certain extent this is a deconstructive (*destruktiv*) approach in the Heideggerian sense: it questions the centeredness of thinking in subjectivity in order to reveal a more fundamental dimension of thought. But at this point the real challenge for thought is not only a deconstruction of a certain modern tradition; the real challenge is to pave new constructive avenues for thought. If part of the issue is an overcoming of subjectivity, the resources for such new avenues cannot be found in yet another rational project that would project new models of explanation on a reality it attempts to change. Instead thinking needs to search for openings through certain attunements to the world in which it arises, and it needs to find again an original commonality with other living and nonliving things. In order to do this, philosophy needs to cease to want to be a science and instead learn to understand itself as an art, as a creative activity that does not fabricate inventions but that draws its creative force from a life that remains its origin.

To explore the bodily dimension in thinking is an exercise in listening and in finding, undoing, and following the threads (the broken ones as well as those that continue) that weave thinking into the fabric of things in their happenings. It is as much an exercise in exploring differences as it is one of concentration, because only in gathering and shaping certain spaces, directions, and motions that animate our thinking in its arising are we able to articulate in speech and writing what comes to thought. This relation between the originating event of thinking and speech appears nicely in a mythical image: Words are what remains attached to the nets that the thinker throws into the open expanse; they are what one brings to the shore.[1]

The bodily dimension that we find in thinking is an ontological dimension: It is an articulation of being; not Being with a capital *B*, but being as an event that is singular and multiple at once and that always occurs bodily. Being is singular when we consider it punctually in its finite happening. No moment of being occurs again in the same way, and each moment of being is tied to a specific constellation of things and events. Being is plural when we consider different things and events in their singularity and interconnections. A tree is, and in that being of the tree there is the leaf that shivers in the wind. There also is the human being that watches the tree and shares the wind that blows through it. There also is a caterpillar moving along a leaf that remains unseen by the human, as well as the distant noise of a nearby highway, hardly perceived. The thinking at play in this description also is, it happens as the movement of the caterpillar happens and the blowing of the wind. But, in distinction to these other events, thinking moves toward an articulation of what comes to awareness in sharing the space of being with other things and events.

The philosophers considered in the present book all offer singular as well as interconnected avenues to think and articulate the event of thinking as an event of bodily being that arises in a world. This is why the explorations of the bodily dimension in thinking in their texts may be viewed as preliminary studies for an ontology of bodily being (hence the title "Concluding Prelude"). There are particular thoughts in each of these philosophers that I find compelling with respect to the possibility of such an ontology and I would like to highlight them again in this concluding prelude.

Plato's *Timaeus* allows us to conceive how an articulation of the difference between a thinking soul and a body comes to be within the movements of a psyche that is bodily and that occurs in a way that mirrors the movements of the stars. In this context the two moments I would like to highlight are, (a) the relation between thinking and the motion of stars, and (b) the relation between thinking, soul, and body.

(a) We saw in the interpretation of the *Timaeus* in chapter 1 that as the movements of the stars return back to recurrent constellations, the movements of the psyche return to the same and thus allow a reasonable discourse to occur. This draws our attention to an aspect of our being and of thinking that is often overlooked, maybe because it becomes more and more difficult to see the stars in the flashing lights of modern technology. In a certain way scientific discourse does acknowledge the influence of the stars in our way of thinking when it comes to physics and mathematics. These sciences are well aware that it has been the movements of the stars that have influenced always anew developments in their fields, since in their motions the stars made space for new models of explanation that paved the way for revolutions in how we think. However, together with these developments, especially in modern science, a living sense of how we share our being with most distant visible and invisible stars, stars that we often see when they already have ceased to exist, has shrunk. The bodily dimension in thinking arises and is shaped within the movement of stars and it would be interesting to follow this thought further and to find ways that are also different from the accounts in the *Timaeus* to think and articulate this occurrence.

(b) One could say that what I try to think with the bodily dimension in thinking is the soul, if we conceive soul in the ancient Greek sense of psyche, and if we interpret this psyche as I did with respect to Plato's *Timaeus*. But as the concept of "body" is burdened by its mechanistic understanding, the concept "soul" is burdened by a Christian tradition, or else it is conceived as fantasy, as some kind of invisible substance that has no hold in reality. But this does not mean that one could not undertake the project of deconstructing these notions of soul and of rethinking soul in its physical quality as the life of things. Similarly to the way in which I developed a notion of body that is not limited to a subject or object but that is a concrete physical dimension of being in which we are interconnected with a world and other beings, the soul too can be understood dynamically as an event that is open to others and otherness.[2] Soul and body could come to name two aspects of the same "thing" in such a way that they name in different ways the "life" of a thing.

What I would like to highlight from the discussion of Nietzsche in chapter 2 is the performativity of thought to which he draws our attention. Nietzsche uncovers the bodily dimension in thinking less in what he writes than in *how* he writes. Certainly how he writes is also tied to what he writes, but in such a way that this "what" is constantly overturned through questions, contradictions, and other rhetorical devices. The two main thoughts I would like to retain from Nietzsche for a possible ontology of bodily being are (a) that the will to power he uncovers is not primarily a human trait, and that (b) chaos is part of being.

(a) Through his particular style Nietzsche makes manifest motions of power and conflicting forces that animate thinking in such a way that this thinking finds itself dispossessed. This leads him to see the struggle of conflicting forces not primarily as a trait of thinking, but as a fundamental trait of all living beings.

(b) Nietzsche makes clear that we cannot grasp life as a whole or the universe as a whole without losing touch with the life we attempt to grasp. In his writing he continuously exposes us to the chaos that belongs to life. Thinking needs to expose itself always anew to this chaos if it wants to regenerate its creative possibilities and if it wants to remain in touch with the fundamental dimension of being that it attempts to think.

There are three issues in Scheler's thought that are of particular interest for an ontology of bodily being: (a) The conception of the body as an analyzer, (b) the idea that the life of thought comes from the most basic emotional impulses that we share with all living things, (c) the idea that what we think cannot be reduced to drives. The first two I have addressed explicitly in chapter 3 and the third is a complementary thought not addressed yet.

(a) Whereas Kant placed the principles of differentiation and synthesis of what we come to think in pure reason, Scheler locates them in the body. In this respect Scheler moves closer to Nietzsche. According to Scheler the body determines if and how I perceive something. Thus it is a threshold to the world, to ourselves, and to other living and nonliving beings. If we do not presuppose a subject to which a body "belongs"—which would go along with the idea that also we become manifest to ourselves only through the body—this opens the possibility for a quite dynamic and also nonsubjective understanding of bodies.

(b) Scheler's thought that the life of our most "elevated" or abstract thoughts entirely comes from the most basic emotional impulses recalls Nietzsche's claim that the most primitive organism expresses will to power. Even if the latest Scheler still maintains a separate principle for spirit, a principle without power, the idea that all life comes from basic emotional impulses opens the way for an ontological conception of being as life-impulse, a conception in which the bodily dimension in thinking shares a basic trait with amoebas that have populated terrestrial oceans far before the appearance of the homo sapiens.

(c) The obstinacy with which Scheler maintains that there is a fundamental difference between what belongs to the psychophysical sphere and what he calls sprit, even when he comes to think spirit in its powerlessness as a negation of reality, promotes further reflection on the originating event of thought. The double principle of thinking (life and spirit) recalls the double origin of the cosmos and of thinking as it is recounted in the *Timaeus*. It points to a moment of rupture or otherness in the arising of ideas that cannot simply be explained with recourse to blind impulses and motions of not yet articulated thoughts. How do we account for the concept that presents itself to our mind as a kind of entity, that is, with a certain stability that allows us to recognize the same concept again and again even if in different ways? It appears to be easier to understand the arising of thought as a bodily event that is accompanied by bodily motions than to think the physicality of a concept that we recognize as in some ways other to this event. Is the consistency of the concept simply in the written or spoken word? A thorough investigation of this question would also need a consideration of memory. I suggested an avenue to understand the arising of concepts that we come to recognize as the same as we think them in chapter 1. Recognition, I suggest, is rooted in repetition; as we recognize recurrent con-

stellations of stars we have recurrent constellations of thought processes with
recurring elements.

Merleau-Ponty's ontology of the flesh (chapter 4) is quite close to the
fundamental issue that animates the present book: bodily being. Questioning
the bodily dimension in thinking leads to an understanding of bodily being that
is not reduced to human thinking or human being but that also points to a dimension of the being of the world we live in and the beings we encounter. This
dimension arises in thought for thought insofar as thinking is bodily woven
into the fabric of things in their happening. Since Merleau-Ponty's thought is
so close to the issue of this book, he opens new avenues for thought precisely
where we find limits in his own accounts. I pointed to these limits at the end of
chapter 4. They concern a focus on the visible (and its invisible) and, related to
this, a predilection of perception as a primary mode of access to the world and
things in the world. However, especially in his latest working notes Merleau-
Ponty moves beyond these limits especially in the thought of the "zero of
being" or the negativity that he thinks as an articulating opening of body,
world, ourselves, and others. In the encounter with openings and limits that I
find in Merleau-Ponty's thought, two issues arise to which I would like to give
further attention: (a) how to think not primarily through visibility, and (b) how
to abandon a binary structure of thought by understanding the negativity at the
center of the chiasm as an opening of multiple entries to the world.

(a) If we close our eyes and try to experience how a blind person would
perceive things, the objective character that we usually attribute to things loses its
clarity. Our fingers glide along the contours of a book that does not become present to us as a thing that is separate from our bodies. Sounds and smells similarly
may pervade us without our being able to locate clearly where they come from.
Vision too may function so that it penetrates the texture of things in such a way
that we feel this texture. Several descriptions by Merleau-Ponty render this
touching quality of senses, so that he does open a language to describe the merging of things and body that does not allow yet a differentiation into subject and
object, but then he moves on to articulate this encounter with things in terms of
a perception that involves two encroaching beings. Besides this possibility of
thinking and articulating perception in different ways, the question is whether
there is not another possible access to bodily being for thought. To a certain
extent, Heidegger (chapter 5) answers this question when he thinks out of a
*Grundstimmung*, a fundamental attunement that is nonvisual and when he thinks
more out of modalities of listening that do not only require our ears but that we
could understand in terms of a certain bodily receptivity that one can exercise.

(b) As for the negativity at the core of the chiasm that for Merleau-
Ponty articulates body and world, me and others, it could mark that moment of

receptivity that has not decided beforehand what it would and what it would not let in. The different sensations and things that may emerge out of an attunement to the negativity through which a world discloses in thinking, do not necessarily present a binary structure. What comes to our awareness in thinking may not refer to a thinking subject at all but may be a multiplicity of concurrent events with which our awareness glides along. A good novel allows for such experiences: we "forget" ourselves as our awareness moves along with a multiplicity of events that emerge from a certain atmosphere that does not yield to a distinction between our reading and what we read. To think bodily being as a multiple event requires that we let go of the intention to think a whole and to grasp something general in thought. It requires also that we let go of the self-reflexive motion that translates all events and things that come to awareness into objects for a perceiving I. What we come to understand as a perceiving I is one of multiple events and things that emerge in the world; it is not always a necessary correlate to what happens (although an awareness must accompany what happens if we want to articulate it in language).

I already have mentioned a couple of elements that I would like to retain from Heidegger's thought for thinking bodily being: attunement and listening. There are two more thoughts from chapter 5 that I will highlight, since they open possibilities to think bodily being and thinking beyond the limits of Heidegger's philosophy: (a) the overcoming of the ontological difference, and (b) Heidegger's thought of time-space as a site where a world discloses.

(a) With the thought of the simultaneity of being and beings, Heidegger opens ways to think things not as objects but out of their being. If we do not want this to lead to a naive positivism, this requires that our understanding of things remain fundamentally attuned to the happening of things; that we practice an attuned listening in which we remain sensitive to the temporality of events and things and to the ways in which their temporality weaves into or resists other temporal events and things. Like other bodies, human bodies, too, retain a thinglike quality and at the same time are experienced and understood as events that weave into and out from the happening of other things in motions of attraction, repulsion, rupture, and going along with.

(b) This understanding of things (bodies) in their happening can be explicated further through the notion of time-space that Heidegger develops in *Contributions*. We saw how being-t/here unfolds as time-space and how this being-t/here is not limited to human modes of being. If our awareness of things arises from attuned modes of being with them, we do not experience things as isolated entities happening in space and *in* time, nor do we get the sense that we project a subjective time onto things. The temporality of a sprout is of that sprout, the temporality of a decaying wall is of that wall, the temporality of a snail is of

that snail. When we thus think the temporality as it occurs with things in difference to other things, this temporality also has a spatial character since it is tied to
a spatial movement. Even a massive thing like a mountain that, as we usually
would say, "does not move," has a peculiar character of motion that we attribute
to it: even a mountain "takes place." This expression "taking place" renders very
nicely how the happening of things is spatial and temporal at once. To think
space and time not separately but as time-spaces that characterize things in their
being, in their taking-place, this is what allows us to think bodies both as things
and as events. It also allows us to explore further the bodily dimension in thinking as a "temporalizing-spatializing" taking-place of thought in relation to things.
Things become mere objects of thought only when we extrapolate their temporality from them, when we abstract them from their concrete happening. Such
operations can of course be useful (science is unthinkable without such operations), but it may be also worth considering what could get lost in these abstrac-
tions. One of the things that get lost is an awareness of the bodily dimension in
thinking, since this dimension appears only in modes of alert bodily being with
other beings.

Foucault's work (chapter 6) is not ontological, although it may be made
fruitful for an ontology. His thought is interesting to the question of the bodily
dimension in thinking especially in two ways: (a) His work points to how our
most intimate thoughts may be formed in practices and institutions that
embody power-knowledge relations that may totally escape our awareness, and
that can never be thought exhaustively, in their totality; and (b) he can be made
fruitful for questioning limits and possibilities of self-reflexive thought.

(a) To a large extent the explorations in this book take a phenomenological approach in a broad sense: They describe what manifests itself (not only vi-
sually) to thinking as thinking reflects its own genesis. Thus the focus is drawn
to certain immediate experiences of coming to presence and passing away, and
also to a lack or negativity that permeate the present moment of thought. This
entails a certain blindness for events in a past that are no longer present, a blindness especially for seemingly marginal events that contribute in shaping our
bodily being. I would like to note that even if Foucault explores marginal events
in history, he limits himself to practices and forms of knowledge of Western history. It may be interesting to investigate how non-Western practices and forms
of knowledge shape present forms of subjectivation, especially since they clearly
have become a part of Western culture. Bodily being is articulated as well by
cultural phenomena like music, art, cinema, and food, all of which import elements for instance from Africa and Asia. I believe that resistances to and assim-
ilations of these elements contribute significantly in shaping not only modes of
subjectivation but ways in which we experience the world.

(b) To bring to awareness so-called foreign elements that already permeate our thoughts and the bodily dimension in thinking requires that philosophy does not limit itself to explicitly reflexive modes of thinking but that it draws impulses from other fields of knowledge as well as from practices that are not only practices of thought (arts, physical activities). Thinking thus moves back and forth between more reflexive motions of thinking and more assimilating motions of thinking. As Merleau-Ponty suggests, a philosophy that does not build on the prejudice of a transcendental subject requires a reflexivity that is rooted in the world, or, to be more precise, in thinking's bodily origination in a world.

An ontology that may arise out of the weaving together of different threads that emerge from the different chapters of this book would not claim universality since it could not overlook the beginning or the end of the threads it weaves together: such an ontology would be enmeshed in them. To a certain extent, this would be a Merleau-Pontinean project, but it would operate more with Heidegger's thought of attunement and being-t/here. At the same time, it would also push farther ahead than Heidegger the thought of a simultaneity of be-ing and beings. This means that this ontology would not operate within the frame of an ontological difference leading to the exploration of first a fundamental ontology and only then, to regional ontologies that are built on it. (Heidegger himself abandons this approach of fundamental ontology in his thought after the thirties when he explores more radically the necessity of sheltering be-ing into beings.) One may say that an ontology of bodily being must be fundamentally regional, and this in at least two different senses: (a) It must be regional as it draws its thoughts from the alertness to concrete modes of being with other beings and as it attempts to remain attuned to these concrete modes of being. (b) It must be regional with respect to current sciences as it neither claims to substitute sciences nor to explain them, nor to ground them. It may explore the ways of bodily being peculiar to different sciences and it may infuse the practice of science with certain sensibilities to issues of being. However I must add that the moral value of these sensibilities would have to remain in question if we do not want to transform this ontology into an ideology that closes off the possibilities that ontological thought can open.

But ontology, even one that is regional in the senses above mentioned, is still an exploration and articulation of fundamental traits of being, and this not only in the sense of a theoretical endeavor that requires a certain systematic approach to its subject. Since an ontology of bodily being requires a certain sensitivity to different forms of being, it also practices a mode of understanding being that arises from and promotes a certain ethos, or way of life. This ethos is marked by a bodily openness and closure of our lives to beings and events in their multiple and encroaching rhythms.

# Notes

## Introduction

1. Note that Merleau-Ponty's notion of "flesh" is a translation of the German "Leib."

2. See, in this respect, Charles Scott's *The Time of Memory* (Albany: State University of New York Press, 1999).

## Chapter 1. On the Origin of the Difference of *Psyche* and *Soma* in Plato's *Timaeus*

1. See Friedrich Nietzsche, "Twilight of the Idols" in: *The Portable Nietzsche*, edited and translated by Walter Kaufmann (New York: Viking, 1982), the section titled "How Finally the True World Became a Fable."

2. Paul Friedländer, *Platon*, vol. 3, Berlin, New York: Walter de Gruyter, 1975, pp. 333 and 355.

3. See A. E. Taylor, *A Commentary on Plato's Timaeus* (Oxford University Press, 1928); F. MacDonald Cornford, *Plato's Cosmology: The Timaeus of Plato*. (London: Routledge and Kegan Paul, 1937). J. N. Findlay, *Plato: The Written and Unwritten Doctrines* (London: Routledge and Kegan, Paul, 1974). Findlay follows Plato's intention to show the primacy of the eidetic principle even so far that he draws the—rather neo-platonic—conclusion that the *Timaeus* "may best be regarded as a comprehensive study in eidetic causation: the self-differentiation of Unity or Ratio or Goodness" (p. 304) in terms of its "descent into instantiation" (p. 305). An exception from these traditional commentaries on the *Timaeus* is certainly John Sallis' work *Chorology* (*Chorology: On Beginning in Plato's Timaeus*, Bloomington: Indiana University Press, 1999).

4. I will refer to two translations of *Timaeus*, the first from *Plato*, Loeb Classical Library, vol. 9, Greek/English, trans. R. G. Bury (Cambridge, MA/London, England: Harvard University Press, 1929), pp. 16–253; the second from *The Collected Dialogues of Plato*, ed. E. Hamilton and H. Cairns (Bollingen Series 71), pp. 1151–1211, trans. B. Jowett.

5. Logos often is equated with rational thought. But this covers over a more original sense of logos that is at play in the *Timaeus* and that will be developed in the following. I will, however, also point to a more restricted sense of logos, when this logos is guided by reason. In this case, I will speak more specifically of "noetic logos."

6. See Paul Friedländer, *Platon*, vol. 1, p. 195. As Sallis nicely states it, through its mythical dimension a dialogue has "within itself a link to the earth, a bond to something intrinsically opaque, a bond to an element of darkness in contrast to that which is capable of being taken up into the light of *logos*." (John Sallis, *Being and Logos: The Way of Platonic Dialogue*, Pittsburgh: Duquesne University Press, 1975, p. 15f.)

7. Timaeus' speech is meant to prepare the later speech of Kritias on the ancient city of Athens; i.e., it is meant to provide an account of the original setting of the nature of the world and of human beings in which the presumed original *polis* of Athens rose.

8. Plato, *Timaeus* 29d–47e.

9. Plato, *Timaeus* 47e–69a.

10. Plato, *Timaeus* 69a–92c.

11. Plato, *Timaeus* 27d–28a.

12. Plato, *Timaeus* 68e.

13. For example the interaction and transmutation between different elements (fire, air, water, earth), the mechanical or accidental cause of movement of bodies, etc., which do not depend in themselves on a divine cause even though it appears that they can be directed in specific ways according to a teleology.

14. Plato, *Timaeus* 48a.

15. Plato, *Timaeus* 29e.

16. Plato, *Timaeus* 30a.

17. Plato, *Timaeus* 30a.

18. Plato, *Timaeus* 49a. Trans. R. G. Bury.

19. Plato, *Timaeus* 50d.

20. Plato, *Timaeus* 51a–b. Trans. B. Jowett.

21. Plato, *Timaeus* 51a–b.

22. Plato, *Timaeus* 51b.

23. Plato, *Timaeus* 69b.

24. I owe the following note to Alejandro A Vallega: "Just as *chora* precedes the physical elements, it may also be said to precede the elements of language, i.e., the letters of the alphabet, which, as Timaeus himself reminds us at the beginning of his second account, share with the physical elements a single name: *estoicheia*." Vide Alejandro A. Vallega, "The Translucence of Words" (unpublished).

25. Plato, *Timaeus* 53a.

26. We surely cannot think of this primordiality of chora as being a period of existence earlier in time than the creation of the world because, as A. E. Taylor points out in his commentary on Plato's *Timaeus*, time comes to be only with the *ouranos* (heaven). But the consequence he draws, that Timaeus just means to say that if you would eliminate God and law, order would vanish (*A Commentary on Plato's Timaeus*, p. 79), simply does not take seriously what Plato writes, and only reduces to logos what essentially escapes logos. That the chora escapes traditional thinking and conceptuality is not reason enough to reinterpret it in terms of traditional thinking and conceptuality.

27. This interpretation of chora is close to the interpretations given by Jacques Derrida in *On the Name*, trans. Ian McLeod (Stanford: Stanford University Press, 1995, pp. 87–127) and by John Sallis in *Chorology* (*Chorology; On Beginning in Plato's Timaeus*, Bloomington: Indiana University Press, 1999) insofar as it differs essentially from traditional interpretations of chora which take chora as being merely the predecessor of the Cartesion *res extensa* (see Taylor's Commentary, p. 312) and insofar as it points to the disruptive character of chora with respect to traditional philosophical discourse.

28. Psyche is commonly translated as "soul." But in order to avoid the misleading connotations associated with this word (as some kind of spiritual entity or subject) I prefer to leave the word untranslated.

29. Plato, *Phaedrus* 245e.

30. Plato, *Phaedo* 105c–d.

31. Plato, *Timaeus* 34a.

32. Plato, *Timaeus* 35a. This translation by R. G. Bury follows the interpretation suggested by A. E. Taylor in his *Commentary* (p. 108). This interpretation differs considerably from Cornford's (see F. MacDonald Cornford,

*Plato's Cosmology*, pp. 63–66). Taylor's interpretation seems more adequate to me for the reasons he exposes in his commentary on p. 108ff.

33. Taylor also points to the connection of the notions of the "Same" and the "Different" with the Pythagorean notions of *apeiron* and *peras* (the infinite and the finite), whose combination is the "unit" (*Commentary*, p. 129). Plato's thought differs from the Pythagorean conception of *stoicheia* (principles) insofar as what for the Pythagoreans was the smallest combination of the two stoicheia, the "unit," in Plato becomes a stoicheia itself (*Commentary*, p. 130). This fact seems to me relevant in the view of Plato's "Ideas," which will be interpreted later as a gathering into one. See also Aristotle, *Met.* A. 986a1–30.

34. See Aristotle in *De Anima* A2, 407b 27f.

35. For the Pythagorean background for this account see Taylor's *Commentary*, pp. 136–46.

36. The outer circle is meant to be "the equatorial circle which is to account for the diurnal revolution of the 'fixed' stars, and this appears to be regular and uniform" (Taylor *Commentary*, p. 149).

37. Plato, *Timaeus* 36b–d; 38c.

38. Plato, *Timaeus* 38b–39e.

39. Plato, *Timaeus* 37a–b.

40. Plato, *Timaeus* 57d–58a.

41. Plato, *Timaeus* 39d.

42. There is a moment where time gathers in the "between," i.e., between a not yet and a not anymore. This is a moment that escapes linear time. This will be elaborated further at the end of this chapter.

43. Plato, *Timaeus* 37a.

44. We may suppose that in this touch a trace of chora is "perceived."

45. Plato, *Timaeus* 27d–28a.

46. I am thinking of the notion "product" not as something "made," but rather, in a literal sense—with reference to the Latin *pro-ducere*—as that which is brought forth.

47. This approach seems to me to be legitimated by the fact that Timaeus says that the creation began when the demiurge took over what was visible but without order and put it into order.

48. Timaeus will speak of the mortal psyche only in the third part of his discourse.

49. Given this "mixture," humans (as we will see) are essentially subject to erroneousness, whereas the legein of the cosmos, Timaeus claims, is always true (37b–c), i.e., it tells the psyche and thus discloses what and how things (ideas and visible bodies) truly are.

50. Plato, *Timaeus* 41d.

51. Plato, *Timaeus* 43ac.

52. Plato, *Timaeus* 43c–d.

53. The courses of the same and the different refer to the immortal psyche that was bound in the head, as Timaeus says in the third part of this discourse. Disorder and disruption are said to occur in the first stage of "incarnation" (childhood).

54. Plato, *Timaeus* 44b.

55. Plato, *Timaeus* 44c.

56. Note that the subject Timaeus talks about is reflected in his approach to the matter.

57. Plato, *Timaeus* 45c–d. Trans. B. Jowett.

58. Timaeus will explain the nature of fire in the second part of his speech where he will trace back the forms of the elements to elementary triangles. (See Taylor, *Commentary* p. 361f.) Among the elements, fire, which is shaped like a pyramid, is the lightest and the most mobile (56a–b). Timaeus describes the transmission of motion through fire in the following manner: "whenever what is naturally mobile is impressed by even a small affection, it transmits it in a circle, the particles passing on to one another this identical impression until they reach the organ of intelligence [*phronimos*] and announce the quality of the agent" (64b) (trans. R. G. Bury).

59. See Bruno Snell, *Die Entdeckung des Geistes*. Studien zur Entstehung des europäischen Denkens bei den Griechen (6., durchges. Aufl., Göttingen, 1986), pp. 16, 18f.

60. Remember that legein also means "to gather."

61. Plato, *Phaedrus*, 249b–c. I am following here John Sallis's translation in *Being and Logos: Reading the Platonic Dialogues* (Bloomington and Indianapolis: Indiana University Press, 3d ed. 1996), p. 149. This passage is crucial also for Sallis insofar as it points to the sense of "gathering" in the Socratic notion of logos. I agree with Sallis that "the 'pre-Socratic' 'experience' of *logos* shows itself in the Platonic writings—thus proving to be not 'pre-Socratic' at all" (*Being and Logos* p. 8).

62. A traditional example of this is the fact that we see a tree *as* tree only if we have in mind the concept "tree." But the interpretation I am giving here takes a different, namely a genetic approach: the "concept" tree originally emerges as one through a gathering of impressions in such a way that, in the gathering, the selfsame differs from the becoming.

63. The middle form is significant here because this means that the psyche is not the subject in the act of collection. Rather she undergoes the occurrence of collection.

64. Plato, *Phaedo*, 67c–d. My translation.

65. This, of course, is much easier to understand if we turn our attention to invisible things. In Timaeus' language we might say that when we think something invisible we think within the already ordered circles of the psyche. Even though in human beings these are always more or less disturbed by sensations of visible bodies and by affections belonging to the mortal parts of the psyche (Timaeus will speak of them only in the third part of his speech), they are certainly far less disturbed than when the perception is enacted primarily from an external body or when it is enacted by human passions.

66. Recall the example Socrates gives in the *Phaedo*: We recognize that two things are similar only if we already have an idea as to what "the similar" is (74e).

67. Sallis explains that "everything can become something said and [. . .] as capable of becoming something said everything is already implicitly gathered into one" (*Being and Logos* p. 151). Further, "the ones must somehow be made available to a seeing" (*Being and Logos* p. 152). But limiting himself to say that ones are already predelineated in logos, Salllis doesn't attempt to give an account on how ones originate. How does the "already there" of a gathering into one come to be?

68. Plato, *Timaeus* 38c–39d.

69. Plato, *Timaeus* 39d–e. Trans. Bury.

70. Plato, *Timaeus* 47b–c.

71. A background for such a reading is given through Augustine's, Husserl's, and Heidegger's analyses of time. (See Augustin's *Confessiones*, book 11; E. Husserl, *Zur Phänomenologie des inneren Zeitbewußtseins* (1893–1917), *Husserlinana*, vol. 10, ed. R. Boehm, Den Haag, 1966, and "Edmund Husserls Vorlesungen zur Phänomenologie des inneren Zeitbewußtseins," ed. Martin Heidegger, in *Jahrbuch für Philosophie und phänomenologische Forschung*, vol. 9 (Halle a.d.S. 1928), pp. 367–497; Martin Heidegger, *Being and Time* 2d part, esp. §§ 65–71 and *Time and Being*).

## Chapter 2. The Return of the Body in Exile: Nietzsche

1. In this context, I am thinking of Martin Heidegger's interpretation of the Greek word "peras" in terms of a limit that gives something free. This means that I understand the word "limit" not simply to name the end of something, but also the beginning. This applies to the thought of both, Plato and Nietzsche.

2. Renée Descartes, "Meditations on First Philosophy," in Descartes, *Selected Philosophical Writings*, trans. John Cottingham, Robert Stoothoff, and Dugald Murdoch (Cambridge: Cambridge University Press, 1933), p. 81f.

3. See Martin Heidegger, *Nietzsche*, vol. 1: "The Will to Power as Art," section 24: "Nietzsche's Overturning of Platonism," pp. 200–10. Heidegger refers to a passage in Nietzsche's *Twilight of the Idols*, entitled "How the 'True World' Finally became a Fable: The History of an Error." This moment of the "twisting free" of metaphysical oppositions is an important issue for contemporary deconstructive thought. See Jacques Derrida's interpretation of the fable in a critique of Heidegger's interpretation in *Spurs: Nietzsche's Styles/Éperons: Les Styles de Nietzsche* (Chicago/London: University of Chicago Press, 1979), p. 70ff; John Sallis, *Force of Imagination: The Sense of the Elemental* (Bloomington: Indiana University Press, 2000), chapter 2B; David Krell, *Infectious Nietzsche* (Bloomington and Indianapolis: Indiana University Press, 1996), p. 1287f.

4. Friedrich Nietzsche, "Twilight of the Idols," in *The Portable Nietzsche*, ed. and trans. Walter Kaufmann (New York: Viking, 1982), p. 486.

5. "1. The true world—attainable for the sage, the pious, the virtuous man; he lives in it, he is it. (The oldest form of the idea, relatively sensible, simple, and persuasive. A circumlocution for the sentence, 'I, Plato, am the truth.'); 2. The true world—unattainable for now, but promised for the sage, the pious, the virtuous man ('for the sinner who repents'). (Progress of the idea: it becomes more subtle, insidious, incomprehensible—it becomes female, it becomes Christian.)" *The Portable Nietzsche*, p. 485.

6. "3. The true world—unattainable, indeterminable, unpromisable; but the very thought of it—a consolation, an obligation, an imperative. (At bottom, the old sun, but seen through mist and skepticism. The idea has become elusive, pale, Nordic, Königsbergian.)" *The Portable Nietzsche*, p. 485.

7. "4. The true world—unattainable? At any rate, unattained. And being unattained, also *unknown*. Consequently, not consoling, redeeming, or obligating: how could something unknown obligate us? (Gray morning. The first dawn of reason. The cockcrow of positivism.)" *The Portable Nietzsche*, p. 485.

8. WP, section 12.

9. Nietzsche distinguishes an active and a passive nihilism (WP, sections 22 and 23).

10. "5. The 'true' world—an idea which is no longer good for anything, not even obligating—an idea which has become useless and superfluous—*consequently*, a refuted idea: let us abolish it! (Bright day; breakfast; return of *bon sens* and cheerfulness; Plato's embarrassed blush; pandemonium of all free spirits.)" *The Portable Nietzsche*, p. 485. "6. The true world—we have abolished. What world has remained? The apparent one perhaps? But no! *With the true world we have also abolished the apparent one.* Noon; moment of the briefest shadow; end of the longest error; high point of humanity; INCIPIT ZARATHUSTRA.)" *The Portable Nietzsche*, p. 485f.

11. Friedrich Nietzsche, *The Gay Science*, trans. Walter Kaufmann (New York: Vintage, 1974), p. 169. In the following cited as GS. German edition: *Die fröhliche Wissenschaft*, in Kritische Studienausgabe [KSA], ed. Giorgio Colli and Mazzino Montinari (Berlin/New York: de Gruyter 1980, vol. 3), p. 471. In the following cited as KSA3.

12. GS, p. 171; KSA3, p. 471.

13. KSA11, p. 161. (My translation.) Compare Kaufmann's translation in Friedrich Nietzsche, *The Will to Power* [WP] (New York: Vintage, 1967), section 476, p. 263. Unless specified, when quoting WP, I refer to the Kaufmann translation.

14. Post. works, KSA13, p. 460. My translation. Compare also the notes from 1888 (post. works, KSA13, p. 53, also in WP, section 477, p. 263f): "I maintain the phenomenality of the *inner* world, too: everything of which we become *conscious* is arranged, simplified, schematized, interpreted."

15. GS, section 333, p. 262. KSA3, p. 559.

16. GS, section 11, p. 84. KSA3, p. 382.

17. GS, section 354. KSA3, p. 592. My translation. Compare GS, p. 299f.

18. WP, section 489, my translation. KSA12, p. 205f.

19. Post. works. KSA11, p. 638, my translation. Compare also the passage in *The Gay Science*, section 333, where Nietzsche writes of that "sudden and violent exhaustion that afflicts all thinkers" and which might have its origin in an unconscious struggle of drives (GS, p. 262; KSA3, p. 559).

20. GS section 333. KSA3, p. 559.

21. Friedrich Nietzsche, *Beyond Good and Evil*, trans. Walter Kaufmann (New York: Vintage, 1989, in the following BGE), section 3, p. 11. KSA5, p. 17.

22. Deleuze describes the will to power as "the genealogical element of force," which means that it is both differential and genetic. The will to power "produces the differences in quantity between two or more forces" and it produces also "the quality due to each force in this relation." (Gilles Deleuze, *Nietzsche and Philosophy*, trans. Hugh Tomlinson, New York: Columbia University Press, 1983, p. 52f.)

23. This seems to be the main thesis of Heidegger when he calls Nietzsche the "accomplisher of metaphysics." I owe a great deal to Heidegger in my understanding of Nietzsche. But I don't follow him when he interprets the moment of the "twisting free" from Platonism as the beginning of the era of technology. I want to go beyond his resistances toward this "twisting free" that he believes to be a moment in which the roots to the truth of being are cut, and suggest that it opens possibilities to grow new roots. Some plants give birth to new ones only by dying.

24. Consider also Eric Blondel's subtle Nietzsche interpretation that shows how Nietzsche's style exceeds metaphysical discourse (*Nietzsche: The Body and Culture: Philosophy as a Philological Genealogy*, trans. Seán Hand, Stanford: Stanford University Press, 1991, p. 7 and p. 19) and lets appear the bodily origin of thinking (p. 35f and 206f).

25. GS, p. 297. Italics added.

26. Nietzsche, GS, section 110, p. 169; KSA3, p. 469f. See also WP, section 493, p. 272; KSA11, p. 506.

27. BGE, section 2, p. 11.

28. Eric Blondel, "'Götzen aushorchen': Versuch einer Genealogie der Genealogie," in *Nietzsche Kontrovers*, ed. R. Berlinger and W. Schrader, Würzburg: Königshausen und Neumann, 1981, p. 51. My translation.

29. In *The Lives of Things* (Bloomington and Indianapolis: Indiana University Press, 2002), Charles Scott calls scientific explanations "metaphors" because they express preconscious and therefore prelinguistic occurrences (*The Lives of Things*, p. 7f). They thus transpose what occurs before consciousness into language. I suspect that for Scott these biological metaphors do not carry any absolute truth claim (although he does claim that they are meaningful), just like for Nietzsche the biological accounts he gives in order to explain the arising of metaphysical concepts can have no more claim to truth than these metaphysical concepts.

30. One may see an affinity, here, between these processes of differentiation and organization in Nietzsche and the differencing/gathering at play in the legein in Plato's *Timaeus*.

31. KSA4, p. 39.

32. KSA4, p. 40.

33. WP, section 485, p. 268.

34. WP, section 481, p. 267.

35. WP, section 492, p. 271.

36. KSA 6, p. 365. My translation.

37. In this context Charles Scott speaks of a self-overcoming in Nietzsche's writing. He analyzes the movement of this self-overcoming in its different aspects in his essay "The Mask of Nietzsche's Self-Overcoming" (in *Nietzsche as Postmodernist, Essays Pro and Contra*, ed. Clayton Koelb, Albany: State University of New York Press, 1990, pp. 217–29). I owe to Charles Scott a great deal of my understanding of the performative character of Nietzsche's thinking.

38. For a more detailed discussion of the relation between the Dionysian and the Apollynian see John Sallis, *Crossing: Nietzsche and the Space of Tragedy*, especially pp. 54–57.

39. *Beyond Good and Evil*, section 13, p. 21; KSA5, p. 27.

40. KSA12, p. 424.

41. KSA13, p. 360.

42. See *The Gay Science*, section 109, p. 168; KSA3, p. 468.

43. *The Portable Nietzsche*, p. 129; KSA4, p. 19.

44. Heidegger developed this thought in his Nietzsche lecture of the summer semester 1937: *Nietzsche's metaphysische Grundstellung im abendländischen Denken: Die ewige Wiederkehr des Gleichen* (Gesamtausgabe vol. 44, ed. M. Heinz, Frankfurt a.M.: Klostermann, 1986). English translation in *Nietzsche*, vol. 1, trans. D. F. Krell. See as well Heidegger's lecture of Bremen: "Wer ist Nietzsche's Zarathustra" of 1953 (in Martin Heidegger, *Vorträge und Aufsätze*, Pfullingen: Neske, 1985). The strength of Heidegger's reading of Nietzsche's thought of the eternal recurrence resides in the fact that he points to the necessity to experience or perform this thought in order to understand it. But I want to distance myself from the direction in which Heidegger interprets Nietzsche's thought, i.e., the interpretation of Nietzsche as the accomplisher of metaphysics and as the forerunner of the era of machination (*Machenschaft*).

45. See Plato's *Phaedo*, 66b–67c.

46. Luce Irigaray, *Marine Lover* (trans. Gillian C. Gill, New York: Columbia University Press, 1991), p. 15ff.

47. Irigaray literally questions Nietzsche in her book and Heidegger expresses in various places that Nietzsche's thought remains still open. See, for instance *Contributions to Philosophy: From Enowning* (trans. K. Maly and P. Emad, Bloomington and Indianapolis: Indiana University Press, 1999), p. 254; German: *Beiträge zur Philosophie: Vom Eregnis* (GA vol. 65, Frankfurt am Main: Vittorio Klostermann, 1989), p. 363, and (*Der Wille zur Macht als Kunst* (GA vol. 43, Frankfurt am Main: Vittorio Klostermann, 1985), p. 283. Here Heidegger writes: "The decisive step of this [*geschichtlich*] reflection must transpose Nietzsche's philosophy into history [*Geschichte*] and thus into the future. And this happens through the recognition upon which all interpretation of this philosophy must be founded: that Nietzsche's philosophy is the *end of Western metaphysics*. This is not intended to be an assertion but it is the leap of being in the transition into the *other* beginning of Western thought that is already set with this end. Only from within the thoughtful preparation of the other beginning can Nietzsche's philosophy be understood as that end and be grasped anew in the path of this transition. [. . .] Probably it will take a long time before Nietzsche will shift from this position of the end of metaphysics into a position of transition. This requires those who see his work in the place where it has opened for itself the new space, yet without being able to freely rebuild itself from the lawfulness [*Gesetzlichkeit*] and ground of this new space." (My translation.) These remarks are in the "Anhang" to vol. 43 of the *Gesamtausgabe*, but not in the translated lecture course "The Will to Power as Art" included in the first volume of *Heidegger: Nietzsche* (Pfullingen: Neske, 1961).

48. As Alejandro Vallega points out in *Heidegger and the Issue of Space: Thinking on Exilic Grounds* (Philadelphia: Penn State University Press, 2003), "*chora* and *chaos* have in common the character of an originary opening" (p. 43) and Aristotle equates chora with chaos in his *Physics* (*Physics*, 4.i, 208b30). Further, in *Metamorphoses* (1. 5ff), Ovid describes chaos "as a mixture of the 'seeds' (semina) or potentialities of all kinds of matter" (*The Oxford Classical Dictionary*, 3d edition, Oxford/New York: Oxford University Press, 1996).

## Chapter 3. Driven Spirit: The Body in Max Scheler's Phenomenology

1. Scheler's phenomenology develops especially through the influence of Husserl's *Logical Investigations* and the phenomenological circle of Munich and Göttingen. Yet it takes its own direction from the very beginning. For a general introduction see also M. Frings, *The Mind of Max Scheler*, chapter 7 (Milwaukee: Marquette University Press, 1997), esp. pp. 181f and 191f.

2. Max Scheler, "Phänomenologie und Erkenntnistheorie," in *Schriften aus dem Nachlass*, vol. 1, Gesammelte Werke, vol. 10, ed. Maria Scheler (Bern, München: Francke, 1957), p. 380. All translations are mine unless specified.

3. Ibid. The German word "*Schauen*" means seeing. In philosophy it is used also to designate a perceiving or a spiritual seeing or vision, i.e., a seeing not with our eyes but more of an intellectual seeing, as Plato may say, with "the eye of the soul."

4. The German word "*erleben*" designates an experience acquired by living. "*Leben*" means to live. The German word for experiencing is "*erfahren*". I will render the word "*erleben*" with "*experience*" but would like the reader to keep in mind the sense of "living through something" which it implies.

5. Ibid.

6. Ibid.

7. Ibid.

8. Ibid.

9. In his phenomenology, Husserl performs two reductions; first he suspends the belief in a reality existing in itself, i.e., he suspends the belief of a world existing in itself; second he performs a "transcendental reduction," i.e., the reduction to transcendental phenomena of consciousness. Scheler does not perform this second reduction.

10. Ibid., p. 394.

11. Ibid.

12. Max Scheler, "Phänomenologie und Erkenntnistheorie," p. 384.

13. Max Scheler, *Der Formalismus in der Ethik und die materiale Wertethik*, Gesammelte Werke vol. 2, ed. Maria Scheler (Bern, München: Francke, 1980), p. 388f. (In English: *Formalism in Ethics and Non-Formal Ethics of Values.*, trans. Manfred S. Frings and Roger L. Funk. Evanston, IL: Northwestern University Press, 1973).

14. Max Scheler, *Die Stellung des Menschen im Kosmos* [SMK] (Bonn: Bouvier 1991), p. 38. (In English: *Man's Place in Nature*, trans. and intro. Hans Meyerhoff. New York: Noonday, 1961). See also *Formalismus*, p. 385; and "Tod und Fortleben" (in *Schriften aus dem Nachlass*, vol. 1) p. 40.

15. Max Scheler, "Phänomenologie und Erkenntnistheorie," p. 398.

16. Ibid., p. 298.

17. I am thinking here especially of Plato's *Phaedo* where Socrates claims that as long as we live we can not reach the pure ideas.

18. The only thing that can never be an object of perception or understanding is the act itself. Acts (the nature of which is spiritual) can be attained only through enactment and never by being objectified.

19. For a more detailed and systematic account of Scheler's understanding of the body in his different works, see the excellent study of Bernhard Lorscheid, *Das Leibphänomen: Eine systematische Darbietung der Schelerschen Wesensschau des Leiblichen in Gegenüberstellung zur Leibontologischen Auffassungen der Gegenwartsphilosophie* (Bonn: Bouvier, 1962).

20. Max Scheler, *Formalismus*, p. 397.

21. The German word *"Abhebung"* has a sense of "elevating from" and thus of letting appear.

22. Max Scheler, *Wesen und Formen der Sympathie* (Bern und München: Francke, 1974), p. 248f. In the following cited as *"Sympathie."* (In English: *The Nature of Sympathy*, trans. Peter Heath. Intro. Werner Stark. London: Routledge and Kegan Paul, 1954. Reprinted Hamden, CN: Archon, 1970).

23. *Formalismus*, p. 410. For Scheler, the inner sense (body) turns out to be the source of our perception of time as a linear movement constituted by past, present, and future. For a more extensive study on the notion of time in Max Scheler see Manfred Frings, *Life Time: Max Scheler's Philosophy of Time* (Dordrecht / Boston / London: Kluwer, *Phaenomenologica Series*, 169, 2003).

24. Max Scheler, *Sympathie* p. 248.

25. See Lorscheid, *Das Leibphänomen*, p. 37f.

26. Max Scheler, *Formalismus*, p. 417.

27. Max Scherler, *Formalismus*, p. 417.

28. Ibid., p. 44.

29. Ibid.

30. Ibid.

31. Max Scheler, SMK, p. 12.

32. Ibid., p. 13.

33. Ibid., p. 17.

34. In *Schriften aus dem Nachlass*, vol. 1, p. 441. For further information about the notion of environment (Umwelt, Milieu) see also B. Lorscheid *Das Leibphänomen*, pp. 72–78.

35. Max Scheler, *Die Stellung des Menschen im Kosmos*, p. 38.

36. Ibid., p. 38f.

37. Ibid., p. 40.

38. Ibid., p. 39.

39. Ibid., p. 40.

40. Ibid.

41. Ibid., p. 38 and *Formalismus*, p. 371.

42. Max Scheler, SMK, p. 40.

43. Ibid., p. 42.

44. Ibid. p. 51.

45. Ibid., pp. 49–51.

46. Ibid., p. 52.

47. For the question of our sense of reality see also Max Scheler, "Erkenntnis und Arbeit," in *Die Wissensformen und die Gesellschaft*.

48. Max Scheler, SMK, p. 54.

49. Ibid., pp. 82–84.

50. Ibid., p. 54.

51. Ibid., p. 55. If one takes into account that inhibition was previously described as a spiritual activity, one might ask whether this anxiety does not arise precisely in the moment of life-negation. But this is not the place to discuss this question further.

52. Ibid., p. 88.

53. Ibid. This description of the birth of metaphysics resembles strikingly Heidegger's account of the rise of the question of being. It is the experience of nothingness that leads to the question of being.

54. Ibid., p. 56.

55. Ibid., p. 56f.

56. Ibid., p. 71.

57. Ibid., p. 67.

58. One who is familiar with Heidegger's *Contributions to Philosophy* will recognize that my description of the spatiotemporal differencing is akin to the occurrence of the "time-space" in the abysmal truth of being as Heidegger attempts to think it.

Chapter 4. Thinking in the Flesh: Merleau-Ponty's
*The Visible and the Invisible*


1. Merleau-Ponty, *Phenomenology of Perception*, trans. Colin Smith (London: Routledge and Kegan Paul, 1962). French version: *Phénoménologie the la Perception* (Paris: Gallimard, 1945).

2. Merleau-Ponty, *The Visible and the Invisible: Followed by Working Notes*, trans. Alfonso Lingis (Evanston, IL: Northwestern University Press, 1968). French version: *Le Visible et L'Invisible: Suivi de Notes de Travail* (Paris: Gallimard, 1964). In the following quoted as "VI," followed by the French pagination and in brackets by the equivalent English pagination.

3. Merleau-Ponty, VI184 [139].

4. Merleau-Ponty, VI195 [149].

5. Merleau-Ponty, VI 52 [31].

6. Merleau-Ponty, VI 53–54.

7. This remark should not discredit a fact of which Merleau-Ponty was very well aware, since it influenced his thought considerably; namely that the later Husserl moved toward an understanding of the world in terms of a life-world that is constituted prepredicatively. See in this context Françoise Dastur's essay "World, Flesh, Vision, in Chiasms: Merleau-Ponty's Notion of Flesh," ed. Fred Evans and Leonard Lawlor (Albany: State University of New York Press, 2000), especially pp. 24–26.

8. This impossibility of thinking to return to its beginning has been thematized and elaborated by John Sallis in *Phenomenology and the Return to the Beginnings* (Pittsburgh: Duquesne University Press, 1973).

9. Merleau-Ponty, VI 57 [35].

10. Merleau-Ponty, VI 60f [38].

11. Merleau-Ponty, VI 28 [12].

12. Merleau-Ponty, VI 58 [36].

13. Note that when I speak of "prereflexive" I do not mean something prior to any kind of awareness but rather prior to reflexive thinking in which an event is articulated *as such*, i.e., prior to the objectification of the event.

14. Merleau-Ponty, VI 61 [38].

15. Merleau-Ponty, VI 61 [38].

16. We share these with animals. That Merleau-Ponty would include animals into this brute perception is suggested also by his courses on "The

Concept of Nature" that are concurrent with the lecture notes of *The Visible and the Invisible*. In his essay "The Indiscernible Joining: Structure, Significa-tion, and Animality in Merleau-Ponty's *La Nature*" (in *Chiasmi International*, vol. 3, 2001), Robert Vallier even suggests that Merleau-Ponty's analyses of animal life play a decisive role in the development of the ontology that we find in *The Visible and the Invisible*.

17. Merleau-Ponty, VI 166 [125].

18. Merleau-Ponty, 167 [125].

19. Compare, in this context, Merleau-Ponty's work note of February 1959 in which he says: "*One cannot make a direct ontology.* My 'indirect' method (being in the beings) is alone conformed with being" (VI 233 [179]). There is, linguistically, no direct access to Being.

20. Merleau-Ponty, VI 209f [158].

21. See the footnote in VI 17 [3]. The translator of the English version was unsure about the translation at this point. "Foi animale," is an expression where "animal" is used as an adjective that designates faith.

22. Merleau-Ponty often vacillates between speaking in terms of foun-dations and denying the appropriateness of these expressions.

23. Merleau-Ponty, VI 210 [158].

24. Merleau-Ponty, VI 152 [113].

25. On the primacy of the percipi, see Henry Maldiney's essay "Flesh and Verb in the Philosophy of Merleau-Ponty," in *Chiasms: Merleau-Ponty's Notion of Flesh* (Albany: State University of New York Press 2000), p. 70.

26. Merleau-Ponty, VI 179 [136].

27. Merelau-Ponty, VI 153 [113f].

28. This description of the act of perception recalls the movement of temporalizing and spacing that we found at play in Scheler's description of the gathering into the I. But whereas Scheler's focus is on the concentration of the I as a spiritual act, Merleau-Ponty focuses on the experience of the self as sen-sible that shares the flesh with the sensible that it encounters and in differenti-ation from which it (the sensible self) emerges.

29. Merleau-Ponty, VI 153[114].

30. Misleading is Merleau-Ponty's expression "no longer" here and in the following sentence. It suggests that first things are a multiplicity of individ-uals synchronically and diachronically distributed and then there is a "spatial

and temporal pulp where things are formed by means of differentiation." It makes sense to think that "no longer" refers to previous, more traditional ways of describing our perception of things, since Merleau-Ponty wants to make the claim that "genealogically," in the order of perception, the differentiation out of homogeneity of perceiver and perceived comes first.

31. Merleau-Ponty, VI 164 [123].

32. Ibid.

33. Merleau-Ponty, VI 191 [146].

34. Merleau-Ponty, VI 302 [248].

35. Merleau-Ponty, VI 184 [140].

36. Merelau-Ponty, VI 153 [114].

37. Merleau-Ponty, VI 153[114].

38. Merleau-Ponty, VI 304 [250].

39. Merleau-Ponty, VI 302 [248f].

40. Merleau-Ponty, VI 191f [146].

41. Merleau-Ponty, VI 165 [123].

42. This is suggested for instance by Luce Irigaray in her critique of Merleau-Ponty. According to Irigaray Merleau-Ponty's analysis is marked by a "labyrinthine solipsism" (*An Ethics of Sexual Difference*, trans. Carolyn Burke and Gillian C. Gill. Ithaca: Cornell University Press, 1993, p. 157) and his notion of reversibility excludes the other: "The reversibility of the world and the I (which Merleau-Ponty refuses to dissociate, to separate into two) suggests some repetition of a prenatal sojourn where the universe and I form a closed economy, which is partly reversible" (*An Ethics of Sexual Difference*, p. 173). I believe that Irigaray's reading of Merleau-Ponty in terms of this solipsism is possible but also reductive of a text that has openings that go well beyond such a reading. A closer look at the gap at the center of reversibility will reveal a negativity and opening to otherness that can no longer be reduced to a solipsistic relation. In regards to the "narcissism," to which Merleau-Ponty points himself with respect to vision (VI 183 [139]), Françoise Dastur already notes in her essay "Merleau-Ponty and Thinking from Within" (in *Merleau-Ponty in Contemporary Perspectives*, ed. Patrick Burke and Jan Van der Veken. Dordrecht/Boston/London: Kluwer, 1993. pp. 3–12) that it is not a solipsism where one recognizes oneself in the spectacle one is looking at, "but quite the opposite, which consists in feeling looked at by things, by an inversion of the look which transforms subjective activity into ontological passivity" (p. 30).

43. Merleau-Ponty, VI 181 [137f].

44. Merleau-Ponty, VI 182 [138].

45. Merleau-Ponty, VI 257 [204].

46. Merleau-Ponty, VI 194f [147–49].

47. This could make the case for a reading that would still see "subjectivism" (or even solipsism as Irigaray claims) to be at play in Merleau-Ponty's thought. However, one should also take into account that through the model of the touching/touched body he finds an opening to an intercorporeal world that includes others precisely in their otherness as well as animals (regarding a man-animality intertwining see Robert Vallier, "The Indiscernible Joining," in *Chiasmi International*, vol. 3, 2001, p. 205).

48. Merleau-Ponty, VI 111 [80].

49. Merleau-Ponty, VI 314 [260].

50. In "Merleau-Ponty aux Limites de la Phénoménologie" (in *Chiasmi International*, vol. 1, 1999) Renaud Barbaras points to Merleau-Ponty's critique of a philosophy that is based on a negativity. Such philosophy results in an objectification of what it questions and thus loses the more fundamental dimension of Being. Barbaras thinks that "to address Being directly, without interposing a nothingness, means that one [Merleau-Ponty] accepts as intrinsic to being a dimension of negativity, since only the threat of a prior nothingness would exclude from Being this negative dimension" (p. 202, my translation).

51. Merleau-Ponty, VI 317 [263].

52. Merleau-Ponty, VI 299 [246].

53. Ibid.

54. Merleau-Ponty, VI 299 [246].

55. Merleau-Ponty, VI 299 [245].

56. Note that reflection is a generative occurrence.

57. Merleau-Ponty, VI 234 [180].

58. See Merleau-Ponty's critique of Sartre in VI 269 [216].

59. See the working note of January 1960, VI 281 [227f]. See also VI 211 [159].

60. Merleau-Ponty, VI 210 [158].

61. Merleau-Ponty, VI 154 [115].

62. Merleau-Ponty, VI 153 [114].

63. Renaud Barbaras uses Deleuze's notion of the "virtual" in order to designate the invisible dimension of Being (the Being of beings) insofar as it is neither pure actuality nor simply potentiality but something in between. He writes: "Le virtuel n'est pas du possible, il est réel en tant que virtuel. [. . .] il existe comme son propre processus d'actualisation" (In *Chiasmi International*, vol. 1, 1999, p. 206).

64. Merleau-Ponty, VI 198 [151].

65. Merleau-Ponty makes this distinction already in *The Prose of the World* (trans. John O'Neill, Evanston, IL: Northwestern University Press, 1973). Here he calls operative language "langage parlant" (translated as "speech") and the secondary language "langage parlé" (translated as "sedimented language").

66. Merleau-Ponty, VI 196 [150].

67. In *De l'être du phénomene* (Grenoble: J. Million, 1991) Barbaras suggests that we might "risk the idea of a chiasm *between the concept of flesh, i.e., of chiasm and of the field of experience that it thematizes*: flesh, as concept, does not reach a nature of things, it remains encompassed by the phenomenal difference that it involves" (335).

68. Merleau-Ponty, VI 200 [153].

69. Merleau-Ponty, VI 202 [154].

70. In "The Thinking of the Sensible" (in *Chiasms*, pp. 121–30) Mauro Carbone quite adequately elaborates the attitude of philosophy that allows for the transposition of the invisible to language as a "letting-be."

71. Merleau-Ponty, VI 200f [153].

72. Many scholars have pointed out the essentially interrogative character of Merleau-Ponty's thinking in *The Visible and the Invisible*. This is not a weakness of Merleau-Ponty but it is rooted in the brute Being he interrogates. As Bernhard Waldenfels writes in "Interrogative Thinking: Reflections on Merleau-Ponty's Later Philosophy": "The region of 'wild Being' presents itself as a region where it is not yet settled once and for all if something is the case, what something is and what it is good for" (*Merleau-Ponty in Contemporary Perspectives*, ed. Patrick Burke and Jan Van der Veken. Dordrecht/ Boston/ London: Kluwer, 1993, p. 5).

73. Merleau-Ponty, VI 105f [75].

Chapter 5.  Bodily Being-T/here:  The Question of Body in the
Horizon of Heidegger's *Contributions to Philosophy*

    1.  *Zollikoner Seminare: Protokolle—Gespräche—Briefe*, ed. Medard Boss
(Frankfurt a. M.: 1987). English translation: *Zollikon Seminars: Protocols—
Conversations—Letters*, ed. Medard Boss, trans. Franz Mayr and Richard Askay
(Evanston, IL: Northwestern University Press, 2001).

    2.  Through the phenomenological movement (Husserl, Scheler) in
German, a distinction was introduced between "Leib" and "Körper." "Leib"
refers to the phenomenological body as it is perceived in internal perception
(*innere Wahrnehmung*), whereas "Körper" indicates the human body as it is represented in the sciences. I will speak of the body more in the first sense.

    3.  "that the corporeal is the most difficult." More precisely, this was an
answer given to a critique Sartre made with reference to the fact that in *Being
and Time* Heidegger only dedicates six lines to the question of the body. *Zollikon Seminars*, p. 231; *Zollikoner Seminare*, p. 292.

    4.  A few remarks in *Being and Time*, trans. Joan Stambough (Albany:
State University of New York Press, 1996. In the following cited as BaT),
pp. 99–101 (German edition: *Sein und Zeit*, Tübingen: Max Niemeyer Verlag,
1984, pp.107–109. In the following cited as SuZ). A little more can be found in
the first lecture of Marburg, *The Metaphysical Foundations of Logic*, trans. Michael
Heim, (Bloomington and Indianapolis: Indiana University Press, 1984), pp.
137–39 (*Metaphysische Anfangsgründe der Logik im Ausgang von Leibniz* (SS 1928),
ed. K. Held, Frankfurt a.M.: Klostermann 1978, GA 26, pp. 173–75.). Then there
are a few pages in the "Letter on 'Humanism,'" in *Pathmarks*, ed. William McNeill
(Cambridge: Cambridge University Press, 1998) pp. 247–48 ("Brief über den 'Humanismus'" in *Wegmarken* (1919–1961), ed. F.-W. von Herrmann, Frankfurt
a.M.: Klostermann 1976, GA 9, pp. 324–26), and a few remarks in *Contributions
to Philosophy (From Enowning)*, trans. Parvis Emad and Kenneth Maly (Bloomington: Indiana University Press, 1999), pp. 37, 194ff, 221, 223, 279 (in the following cited as C) (*Beiträge zur Philosophie (Vom Ereignis)*, 1936–1938, ed. F.-W.
von Herrmann, Frankfurt a.M.: 1989, GA 65, pp. 53, 275ff, 314, 318, 399). Most
can be found in the *Seminars of Zollikon*. (Heidegger's works from the complete
edition hereafter cited with reference to the volume: GA . . .)

    5.  Heidegger, BaT, p. 14 ; SuZ, p. 15.

    6.  See Heidegger, C, sections 107, 132, 258, 266, pp. 144f, 176f, 297ff,
327–30; GA 65, pp. 207, 250f, 423f, 466–46.

    7.  For a more detailed introduction to *Contributions*, see my *Heidegger's
Contributions to Philosophy: An Introduction* (Bloomington: Indiana University Press, 2003).

8. See F.-W. v. Herrmann, *Heideggers "Grundprobleme der Phänomenologie": Zur "Zweiten Hälfte" von "Sein und Zeit,"* Frankfurt a.M.: 1991. For the transition from *Being and Time* to *Contributions to Philosophy*, see also the first part of my *Heidegger's* Contributions to Philosophy: *An Introduction* (Bloomington: Indiana University Press, 2003).

9. Martin Heidegger, *The Metaphysical Foundations of Logic*, p. 137f; GA 26, p. 172f.

10. Martin Heidegger, "Letter on 'Humanism,'" in *Pathmarks*, p. 250; GA 9, p. 328; C, p. 317, GA 65, p. 450f. See also *The Basic Problems of Phenomenology*, trans. Albert Hofstadter (Bloomington and Indianapolis: Indiana University Press, 1988), p. 322f; GA 24, p. 459.

11. Martin Heidegger, *The Fundamental Concepts of Metaphysics: World, Finitude, Solitude*, trans. William McNeill and Nicholas Walker (Bloomington and Indianapolis: Indiana University Press, 1996); GA 29/30: *Grundbegriffe der Metaphysik: Welt—Endlichkeit—Einsamkeit* (WS 1929/30), Hrsg. F.-W. von Herrmann (Klostermann: Frankfurt a.M.: Klostermann 1992$^2$).

12. Heidegger, C, p. 11, GA 65, p. 14f.

13. Heidegger, C, p. 75, GA 65, p. 108.

14. See Martin Heidegger, *Introduction to Metaphysics*, trans. Gregory Fried and Richard Polt (New Haven: Yale University Press, 2000), pp. 190–202; GA 40, pp. 189–97.

15. In German, "Ent-setzen" usually means startled dismay or fright as well. But literally it means to "set out" or "being set out." In section 269 of *Contributions* Heidegger speaks about it as the "*Aufriss des Stimmungshaften selbst*" (C, p. 340, GA 65, p. 483), a rift that opens originally the basic attunements.

16. Heidegger, C, p. 12, GA 65, p. 15f.

17. I did not make this analogy between the experience of death and the experience of an epochal withdrawal of be-ing by accident. Heidegger points to the relation between the two occurrences himself. In *Contributions* he says that the original self-concealment of truth is mirrored in the way humans relate to death (C, p. 227f, GA 65, p. 324f).

18. Since the very origin of thinking is something that overcomes us and we "only" respond to what is revealed to us, we humans appear to be in a quite "passive" and "powerless" position. The only thing we can do, it seems, is to gather in silence toward being's withdrawal, to think its history in order to experience its abandonment in our present era. This is why many interpreters see a nihilistic trait in Heidegger's thinking. See, for instance, Michel Haar who in his book *Heidegger et l'essence de l'homme* (Grenoble: Millon 1990) claims that finally in

Heidegger's thought humans are more and more deprived of their faculties (p. 171), or Constantino Esposito who in his book *Heidegger: Storia e Fenomenologia del Possibile* (Bari: Levante 1992) interprets being as that "which refuses itself to any realization," as "original impotency that marks anything that is" (p. 9). He also affirms that since "we can not get out of metaphysics by a strike of will [. . .] the remembering can not but think the inevitability, the absolute necessity of oblivion" (p. 326). (My translations.) But these nihilistic views of Heidegger's thinking often have a tendency to see being and humans in opposition or they do not see how far this thought thinks in the "simultaneity" of being and beings.

19. Heidegger, C, pp. 6, 17, GA 65, pp. 7, 23–24. See F.-W. v. Herrmann, *Wege ins Ereignis: Zu Heideggers "Beiträgen zur Philosophie"* (Frankfurt a.M.: Klostermann 1994), pp. 30–31.

20. Heidegger often uses the word *"Verwahrung," "*safe-keeping," synonymously with *Bergung.* In its literal sense *Ver-wahrung* (*"wahr"* means "true") means: to bring into truth.

21. The essay is published in GA 5, pp. 1–74. English translation in Martin Heidegger, *Basic Writings,* revised and expanded edition, ed. D. F. Krell (San Francisco: Harper, 1993), pp. 139–212; in the following referred to as "BW, p. . . ." The reference to "The Origin of the Work of Art" is on p. 274 of *Contributions* (GA 65, p. 392).

22. See also Heidegger's lecture on Hölderlin of the winter semester 34/35, GA 39, p. 144.

23. Heidegger, GA 65, p. 391. In the thirties Heidegger insists on the distinction between the strife between world and earth on the one hand and concealment and unconcealment on the other hand. Yet in the thinking of the "fourfold" (*Geviertsdenken*), where he thinks being as the relation between gods and mortals, sky and earth, this distinction is no longer made. Indeed Heidegger moves toward a thinking that incorporates more and more the "simultaneity" of being and beings.

24. Heidegger, BW, pp. 167, 170; GA 5, pp. 28, 31.

25. Heidegger, GA 5, p. 28; BW, p. 168.

26. Heidegger, BW, p. 171; GA 5, p. 32.

27. In *The Song of the Earth: Heidegger and the Grounds of the History of Being,* trans. Reginald Lilly (Bloomington: Indiana University Press, 1993), Michel Haar distinguishes four senses of earth: (1) earth has an ontological sense akin to the withdrawal of be-ing; it is that which in its emerging keeps its own depth hidden; (2) earth in the sense of nature (phusis); (3) earth as the "matter" of a work of art; (4) earth as the land of a people (pp. 57–64). Of these four senses I mentioned only the second and the third.

28. Heidegger, GA 5, p. 33.

29. Heidegger, GA 5, p. 35.

30. Heidegger, BW, p. 186; GA 5, p. 48.

31. See, Heidegger's "On the Origin of The Work of Art," in *Basic Problems*, p. 178f, where Heidegger speaks of the concealment in the first sense as *Versagen* (refusal) and in the second sense as *Verstellen* (dissembling); GA 5, p. 40f. In the conference "On the Essence of Truth" he speaks about it as *Geheimnis* (mystery) and *Irre* (errancy) (in *Pathmarks*, pp. 148–51; GA 9, pp. 193–98.)

32. See Max Scheler, *Wesen und Formen der Sympathie* (Bern: Francke, 1974), especially pp. 232–58, here p. 255.

33. Unfortunately, the German word "*leibhaftig*" cannot be properly translated. It entails not only the sense of "bodily" but also of "truly." For instance we say: "Sie war leibhaftig anwesend": "She was truly present, in bones and flesh."

34. Whether the corporeality of animals and plants is open to the original concealment of be-ing is a question for further inquiry.

35. Heidegger, BW, p. 359; "Bauen, Wohnen, Denken," in *Vorträge und Aufsätze* (Pfullingen: Neske, 1954; in the following cited as VA), p. 152.

36. Heidegger, BW, p. 358; VA, p. 151.

37. See *Zollikon Seminars*, p. 196; *Zollikoner Seminare*, p. 244. Note that Heidegger uses here the language of *Being and Time*.

38. Heidegger uses the word "Gegenwurf" in his "Letter on 'Humanism,'" p. 260; "Brief über den Humanismus," in *Wegmarken*, GA 9, p. 342.

39. Already in *Being and Time* (section 26) Heidegger makes clear that Dasein includes *Mitsein*, i.e., being with others.

40. The reader may be interested to know that I worked on the question of body in Heidegger before working on Merleau-Ponty's notion of flesh.

41. One should suppose that there even is a connection between what Heidegger experiences as a historical necessity and the fact that he has not pursued more explicitly the question of bodily being. But to explore this adequately we would need further analyses.

42. For the specific role of language in *Contributions* see my essay "Poietic Saying" in *Companion to Heidegger's* Contributions to Philosophy, eds. Charles Scott, Susan Schoenbohm, Daniela Vallega-Neu, and Alejandro Vallega (Bloomington: Indiana University Press, 2001), pp. 67–70.

43. The elaboration of the relation between a disclosive bodily ek-stasis and a concealing excitement would require further and more detailed analyses that I rather reserve for a future project.

44. I have developed the issue of the decision in which Heidegger's thinking of *Contributions* is caught in my essay "Thinking In-Decision" (in *Research in Phenomenology*, 2003).

## Chapter 6. Exorbitant Gazes: On Foucault's Genealogies of Bodies

1. Charles E Scott, *The Question of Ethics: Nietzsche, Foucault, Heidegger* (Bloomington: Indiana University Press, 1990), p. 63.

2. "The ethics of care for the self as a practice of freedom," p. 10. This interview appeared in *The Final Foucault*, ed. James William Bernauer and David M. Rasmussen (Cambridge: MIT Press, 1988

3. Michel Foucault, *Discipline and Punish: The Birth of the Prison*, trans. Alan Sheridan (New York: Vintage, 1995).

4. Michel Foucault. *The History of Sexuality: An Introduction*, trans. Robert Hurley (New York: Vintage, 1990).

5. Michel Foucault, "Truth and Power," in *Power/Knowledge: Selected Interviews and Other Writings 1972–1977*, ed. Colin Gordon (New York: Pantheon, 1980), p. 117.

6. Michel Foucault, "The Subject and Power," in Hubert L. Dreyfus and Paul Rabinow, *Michel Foucault: Beyond Structuralism and Hermeneutics* (Chicago: University of Chicago Press, 1982), p. 208.

7. Michel Foucault, "Nietzsche, Genealogy, History," in *Language, Counter-Memory, Practice: Selected Essays and Interviews by Michel Foucault*, ed. Donald F. Bouchard (Ithaca: Cornell University Press, 1977), p. 156.

8. *Power/Knowledge*, p. 193.

9. Ibid.

10. Foucault defines truth as follows: "Truth is a thing of this world: it is produced only by virtue of multiple forms of constraints. And it induces regular effects of power. Each society has its regime of truth, its 'general politics' of truth: that is, the types of discourse which it accepts and makes function as true; the mechanisms and instances which enable one to distinguish true and false statements, the means by which each is sanctioned; the techniques and procedures accorded value in the acquisition of truth; the status of those who are charges with saying what counts as true" (*Power/Knowledge*, p. 131).

11. See Charles E. Scott, *The Question of Ethics*, chapter 3: "Ethics Is the Question: The Fragmented Subject in Foucault's Genealogy," pp. 53–93.

12. Friedrich Nietzsche, *The Will to Power*, trans. Walter Kaufmann and R. J. Hollingdale (New York: Vintage, 1968), fragment # 492, p. 271.

13. Nietzsche, *The Will to Power*, # 485, p. 268.

14. *Michel Foucault: Beyond Structuralism and Hermeneutics*, p. 220.

15. Ibid., p. 220.

16. *Discipline and Punish*, p. 29.

17. *Power/Knowledge*, p. 186.

18. Gilles Deleuze, *Foucault*, trans. Sean Hand (Minneapolis, London: University of Minnesota Press, 1995), p. 94.

19. Deleuze, *Foucault*, p. 94. Diagrams are abstract mechanisms that define power-knowledge relations independently form specific contents. Panopticism would be an example for a diagram (see *Discipline and Punish*, p. 205).

20. Deleuze, *Foucault*, p. 96.

21. Deleuze, *Foucault*, p. 114.

22. Deleuze, *Foucault*, p. 116.

23. Deleuze, *Foucault*, p. 117.

24. Deleuze, *Foucault*, p. 117.

25. "The Ethic of Care of the Self as a Practice of Freedom," in *The Final Foucault*, p. 2.

26. *The Final Foucault*, p. 18.

27. *The Final Foucault*, p. 12f.

28. Michel Foucault, *The Care of the Self: The History of Sexuality, Volume 3* (HS3) (New York: Vintage: 1988), p. 66. According to Pierre Hadot though, Foucault misinterprets Seneca at this point. Hadot says that Foucault fails to make an important distinction between pleasure and joy: "In the twenty-third letter, Seneca is in fact explicitly contrasting *voluptas* and *gaudium*, pleasure and joy; and one cannot therefore speak, as Foucault does (p. 83), on the subject of joy, of 'another form of pleasure'." Further Foucault does not make important distinctions with regard to the self: "the Stoics did not find joy in the 'self' but, as Seneca says, 'in the best part of the self,' in the 'true good' (Seneca, letter XXIII, 6) . . . The stoic exercise aims in fact at going beyond the self." ("Reflections on the notion of 'the

cultivation of the self'," in *Michel Foucault Philosophe*, New York: Routledge, 1992, p. 226.) This criticism by Hadot is interesting because it sheds a light on some of Foucault's interpretative moves, i.e., we see how in the stoic texts he looks for possibilities of practices of care of the self that do not presuppose a spiritual self that operates outside of the economy of power-knowledge relations.

29.  Foucault, HS3, p. 124.

30.  Foucault, HS3, p. 52f.

## Concluding Prelude

1.  See Alejandro A. Vallega, *Heidegger and the Issue of Space: Thinking on Exilic Grounds* (Philadelphia: Penn State University Press, 2003), p. 25.

2.  Julia Kristeva did some work on the notion of soul in its psychoanalytical aspect that could be helpful for such a project. See her book *New Maladies of the Soul*, trans. Ross Guberman (New York: Columbia University Press, 1995).

# Index

Scheler, Max, xvii, 40–41, chap. 3, 59, 94, 123–124, 144n28
Schopenhauer, 28
Scott, Charles, 30, 104, 129n2, 137n29, 138n37, 153n11
Sensible, 79
Sheltering, 90–94
Snell, Bruno, 133n59
Soul, 22, 110, 123. *See also* psyche
Spirit, 45, 50, 53, 55–57; in distinction to body, 48–49, 50
Strife between world and earth, 92–93, 150n23
Subject, 106, 108–109; as product, 31–32; dispossessed, 112; in relation to truth, 104; transformation of, 108. *See also* subjectification
Subjectification, 106, 108, 111

Taylor, A.E., 129n3, 131n26, 131n32, 132n33
Thinking/thought, xv, 122–123; from the outside, 104–106; incep-
tual, 86; performative 28–29, 31, 51; productive/originating, 31; reflexive 60–64
Time, 17–18, 132n42, 134n71
Time-space, 126–127, 142n58; of things, 66–67
Truth 102, 104, 107–108, 118, 152n10; of be-ing, 86, 93–94. *See also* concealment

Unconscious part of thinking, 30–31.

Vallega, Alejandro, 131n24, 139n48, 154n1
Vallier, Robert, 144n16, 146n47
Vision, primacy of, 77
Vital sphere, 52–53, 125

Waldenfels, Bernhard, 147n72
Will to power, 28, 33–35
World, 93, 95; brute, 60, 64